WARBIRDS WORLDWIDE - THE LEADER IN I

Top: *The Dutch Spitfire Flight's MK732, featured in WW 28, seen here in its new D Day commemorative paint scheme as OU-U and looking very combat like when* **Richard Paver** *took the photograph on May 8th - Dan Griffith is at the controls. The Dutch Air Force are fully supporting the operation of MK732 as a tribute to all those that serviced and flew the type in World War II.* ***Below:*** *in complete contrast, Victoria Air Maintenance undertook the rebuild of Richard Sugden's unique T-2B Buckeye N212TB in Canada* **(Grant Hopkins VAM)**

JOURNAL No. 29

Editorial (Tel: 0623 845551 Fax 0623 845556)

Founders Paul A. Coggan, John R. Sandberg, Henry J. 'Butch' Schroeder III

Editorial Director Paul A. Coggan

Editorial Address: P.O. Box 99., Mansfield, Notts NG19 9GU, ENGLAND
North American Office: Midwest Aviation Museum
RR6 Box 325 Danville IL 61832 USA

Financial Adviser: Philip Warner F.C.A.

Warbird Insurance Adviser: Nigel Foster (Edgar Hamilton Ltd.)

Technical Illustrator: Terry Lawless

International Chief Photographer Thierry Thomassin

Chief Pilot Mark Hanna (Old Flying Machine Co.)

Historical Researcher Mark Sheppard

Book Reviews & Main Feature ideas James Kightly

Video Reviews Gary R. Brown

Correspondents
Peter Anderson (Australia)
Ian Brodie (New Zealand)
Gary Brown (UK)
Duncan Curtis (UK)
Joe Cupido (USA)
Robert DeGroat (USA)
John Dibbs (UK)
Jeff Ethell (USA)
Erich Gandet (Switzerland)
Alan Gruening (USA)
Mike Hodson (USA)
Paolo Franzini (Italy)
Craig Justo (Australia)
Michael Kroger (Germany)
Frank Mormillo (USA)
Derek Macphail (UK)
Richard Paver (UK)
Dick Phillips (USA)
Bruce Potts (Australia)
Sharon Sandberg (USA)
Tom Smith (USA)

Advertising Call (0623) 845551 for rates
or Fax (0623) 845556 for a rate card. U.S. Representative Michael J. Raftus
(508) 429 4958 or Fax (508) 429 5804

Articles and photographs for consideration should be sent to the Editor at the above Editorial address. For major features please send an outline first. Opinions expressed by our contributors are not necessarily those of Warbirds Worldwide Ltd.

SUBSCRIPTION INFORMATION

Warbirds Worldwide is available on subscription: UK £18.50, REST OF EUROPE £21.00- USA $44.00, Canada $C48.00, Australia $A49.00, New Zealand NZ$59.00 Hong Kong £24.00. Asia £24.00 We accept VISA, MASTERCARD, and AMEX or you can pay by personal cheque in local currency. For Europe Eurocheques are preferred. Please send fee to above address (Please note we have an office in North America) or Fax credit card details to (0623)845556 telling us which copy you wish to start with. All publications are sent by *Air Mail* in card envelopes. *Get it First Get it Fast - subscribe today!*

VIEWPOINT

Many of you will have already recognised the above aircraft as Golden Apple Trust's F-86A G-SABR/48-0178, now being operated on their behalf by the Old Flying Machine Company. The background to this and more pictures of the aircraft today in WW30. (Duncan Curtis)

Well, the 1994 flying season in the Northern hemisphere is here and it's time to slap on the suncream (or barrier cream depending on your outlook) and brave the UV's for another years exciting flying. In preparing the new section *Industry News* it came home to me just how much activity there is worldwide. Everywhere. From Rhode Island to Romania, warbirds are being rebuilt in every shape and size, to varying standards from good through to excellent. Even now I still get excited at seeing the prospect of a new type take to the air. After the recent prospect of the FAA grounding the U.S. based warbird population it comes as a relief to hear things are more stable. All over the world various authorities are taking more interest in warbird - ex military aircraft being operated by civilians - generally because the numbers are growing rapidly. Also no doubt because there is money to be made from certificating and regulating them. The saying 'safety in numbers' springs to mind. With growing numbers of aircraft and therefore owners, operators and engineering operations there is a much more powerful movement to resist *unfair* over regulation. One operator in the U.S.A. said to me recently "...the FAA had no option but to back down, because if they didn't the whole warbird air force would have armed up and bombed the shit out of every FAA installation for miles around." A colourful expression of the weight of feeling no doubt: not quite how I saw the situation, but it is more difficult now than it has been in the past to enforce unfair over regulation and discriminate against warbird owners. Long may it continue. It is certain that there is safety in numbers in one way, but in others, particularly where statistics are concerned there will be more accidents. National (and international) media jump at every opportunity to report on spectacular mishaps and accidents. It sells newspapers, and increases viewing figures. If you are involved in an accident or incident you would do well to avoid contact with the national media, especially where they are likely to make the whole warbird movement look like a load of lunatics with more money than sense. All the more reason to concentrate on those checks this year and fly safe. And live in hope that the media report on your activities for the right reasons.

I have been asked to point out that the filter fitted to Bf109G2 *Black 6* had not flown on the aircraft as we reported in *Warbirds Worldwide 28* (we were misinformed) and is in fact inoperable in its current form. Hope that puts the record straight. Have a good one! WW Paul Coggan

SEE THE WARBIRDS WORLDWIDE STAND (48) AT DUXFORD:
- OFMC Flying Day 26th June 1994
- Flying Legends 16/17th July
- Autumn Air Day 16th October

CONTENTS

6 INDUSTRY NEWS
There has *never* been so much activity surrounding warbird aeroplanes - our new initiative brings you up to date on *some* of this activity! We start on Page 6 with general news, the latest on CAA and FAA activity, *Jet Reports* (P18) and an update on *Victoria Air Maintenance* (P19): a full ten pages of in depth, accurate information.

16 Flying Legends
Paul Coggan previews the forthcoming *Flying Legends Airshow* at Duxford;the event that will remind aficianados of how they came to be seduced by warbirds!

20 TEXAS 262's
We report on the latest initiative from *Classic Fighter Industries* and *Texas Airplane Factory* in Fort Worth - the manufacture of Me262s based on information from *CFI's* VP, *Charles Searock*.

24 Anachronistic Swordfish
James Kightly on the current status of the world's Swordfish population as an introduction to our major features on this Naval biplane

27 SHEARWATER SWORDFISH
John Beattie takes us to Canada and gives a first hand account of test flying Shearwater's newly rebuilt Swordfish.

34 Fishbed 21
Peter N. Anderson writes about the *Sonic Aviation Syndicate's* beautiful MiG-21 Fishbed now fully operational downunder.

38 RED SAILOR'S Bf110
Mark Sheppard, tells the story of *The Alpine Fighter Collection's* Bf110. *Exclusive colour profile* by WW's *Terry Lawless* on Page 43.

44 Hawker Fury
Richard Paver photographs John Bradshaw's ex Iraqi Hawker Fury and tells the story of acquiring and operating the type.

48 FILMING 633 SQUADRON
Gary R. Brown tells the story of the filming of Mirisch Films 633 Squadron and Mosquito Squadron in the first of a series on warbird action in the movies.

> We run **Thierry Thomassin's** feature on the *Yanks Air Museum* - **James Kightly** covers the story of *Ernie Van Simmons*, Canadian collector - *Warbirds over Wanaka '94* - a report by **Jim Winchester** - **Paul Coggan** interviews Tim Wallis about the future of the *Alpine Fighter Collection* - **John Dibbs** takes an in depth look at Charles Darby and Jim Pavitt's NZ based Harvard - **Frank Mormillo** chronicles the P-40 as a warbird in the USA - **Mark Hanna** writes about flying the *Hawker Fury* and **Paul Coggan** interviews *Robert Lamplough* - one of Great Britain's first warbird owners.
> **Available end of August 1994**

The Flying Insurance Broker - see page 58

Industry News

CFS AEROPRODUCTS UK LAUNCH

Just past the Coventry airport complex at Baginton and nestling in the *Alvis Works* is *CFS Aeroproducts*. Despite the fact the company have only recently formed in the U.K. the experience level at the new company is impressive. In one of the former Alvis Leonides Aero Engine buildings a new custom built facility is in the final stages of completion. Essentially the company specialises in the overhaul and repair of Pratt & Whitney radial piston engines, Hamilton Standard propellers and aircraft/engine accessories. With a growing warbird and Dakota fleet in the U.K. and Europe as well as potential business opportunities overseas *CFS Aeroproducts* are set to move into this growing field.

The history of the company goes back much further than its new formation date. Essentially *CFS* have taken over the Maltese company *CFS Aero Engines* which itself has an interesting history. In 1967 the American company *Miarco* was employing 140 people in Malta, looking after the needs of some 20 to 30 aircraft operating in the area. The mid 1980s saw business slowing down and the airframe company was sold to *NCA* but the Maltese government kept the engine overhaul business going. Renamed *CFS Aero Engines* the company was tasked with looking after the needs of the growing fleet of DC-3s of *Air Atlantique*.

In September 1993 the decision was taken to move the company to the U.K. to support the flight operations of *Air Atlantique* closer to home. Essentially the brief for the new U.K. based company, renamed *CFS Aeroproducts* (to reflect its involvement with other services) was to supply all the facilities offered by the Maltese organisation but with a more efficient workforce and to broaden its customer base. CFS Director Martin Slater told *Warbirds Worldwide* ... "the building we now occupy was built in

Above: CFS Aeroproducts propeller shop at the Alvis Works close to Coventry airport. The company's main activities involve Pratt & Whitney aero engine overhaul (Martin Slater).

1978 and there are some engine test cells just down the road which we hope to be able to utilise at some stage once we are fully operational here". The building was literally an empty shell when the *CFS* team moved in. It is now being configured to accept engines in at one end and pass along the line undergoing tear down, cleaning, inspection and NDT, overhaul, reassembly and eventually testing and out of the door. The main business will be the overhaul and rebuilding of all Pratt & Whitney radials i.e. R985,R1340,R1830,R2000 and R2800s in addition to all Hamilton Standard Propellers and accessories that go with the engines and in some cases airframes. Martin went on to say " ...it is our intention to set off on the right foot, to make full use of our teams expertise with overhauling and troubleshooting P&W piston engines, their propellers and accessories". *CFS* are already doing work for *Aero Rebuild* in South Africa, the *Dutch Dakota Association*, *Palfe* (Spain), *Classic Air* (Switzerland) *Old Flying Machine Company* at Duxford, and several other aircraft operations in Sweden, Norway, Finland and India and of course for *Air Atlantique*.

As we close for press the new building is nearing completion and there are already a number of engines and propellers being processed. *Warbirds Worldwide* will pay a more formal visit once *CFS* are fully operational. Anyone requiring further information on the services being offered by *CFS Aeroproducts* should contact Martin Slater direct on 0203 305873 or by Fax on 0203 302088 (report by Paul Coggan)

ROMANIAN YAK-11 FIRST FLIGHT

Alain Capel of the French based *Capel Aviation* contacted *Warbirds Worldwide* as we went to press to announce the first flight of the company's Yak 11 -the first of ten being rebuilt (one ex Egyptian airframe and several ex Romanian Air Force machines)at their facility in Romania. Californian based Yak pilot Joe Haley was the test pilot and the first flight occurred on the evening of 15th April - the 45 minute flight went very smoothly, with the aircraft in RomAF colours appropriately coded 01. This is a major milestone for *Capel Aviation*, and other warbirds are now scheduled to be shipped to Romania for rebuild at their facility (Paul Coggan report via Alain Capel).

PAPERWORK

WARNING: The following is for information only and should not be regarded as a substitute for official information released by appropriate aviation authorities in any country.

The following letter was released by the U.K. Civil Aviation Authority in April 1994:

"DOWTY ROTOL VINTAGE PROPELLERS (SPITFIRES AND HURRICANES)

The Civil Aviation Authority has reason to suspect that replacement wooden blades for certain vintage Rotol propellers may be unapproved parts. The replacement blades are manufactured by Hoffman and should have been released for service via Dowty Aerospace Propellers (DAP). However, certain propeller blades may have found their way into the UK via other routes.

The propellers are used on Spitfire and Hurricane aircraft.

DAP Drawing No.   Hoffman No.
600013583   VP10-412
600014789   VP10-505
600015027   VP10-568
600015313   VP10-722

The attachment lists all blades which have been manufactured by Hoffman and subsequently inspected and released by Dowty. Blades which are NOT on the list must be considered unapproved. Please refer to the CAA Powerplant Department (telephone 0293 573196)where any doubt exists as to any particular blade."

A letter from the CAA's Safety Regulation Group to many warbird operators suggests the CAA is concerned about N registered aircraft continuing to operate in the U.K. on documents other than the Standard CofA. The letter reads:

Above: From Alain Capel comes the marvellous photographs of the first Yak-11 to be rebuilt in Romania taking to the air for its first post rebuild flight on April 15th.

"The Civil Aviation Authority and Federal Aviation Authority are concerned regarding American registered aircraft flying within UK airspace on a document other than a Standard Certificate of Airworthiness.

This concern mainly relates to the validity of the Special Airworthiness Certificate and the operating limitations together with the control of basic airworthiness standards.

It has been agreed that prior to the next renewal of any UK (ART 7) Exemption which is based on the validity of the U.S. documents, the applicant will need to supply to the Civil Aviation Authority written confirmation from the Federal Aviation Administration that the said documents are currently valid and applicable for operation in the UK. Confirmation from the Federal Aviation Administration will not be required annually, but documents will be verified by the Civil Aviation Authority.

Where an Exemption is required to be renewed within the next month (this letter was dated 9th March 94) the Civil Aviation Authority will undertake the renewal based on the current US documents. However, the following renewal will require compliance with the aforementioned procedure".

LETTER TO OWNERS/OPERATORS NO 1333 VICKERS SUPERMARINE SPITFIRE AIRCRAFT ALL MARKS EXCEPT XVIII SPAR BOOMS REMANUFACTURED FROM L105.
The following letter was sent from the CAA to Spitfire owners/operators early in March 94

"Replacement of original spar booms constructed of nested square tubes of L63 with booms constructed of L105 had been accepted on an early restoration (to Trent Aero Mod 613). Recent analysis has shown that this results in a wing of insufficient strength over parts of the manoeuvring envelope, furthermore many other Spitfires have had similar material replacements during their restoration. The CAA has reviewed the analysis data and requires, as a condition of the CAA Permit to Fly, that the following actions be taken on all Spitfire marks, except XVIII, which have had spar booms remanufactured from L105 in lieu of original L63. Before further flight, unless more restrictive limitations are already applicable to specific aircraft, all Spitfires must have a placard installed in the cockpit, in full view of the pilot stating:
i) Aerobatics are prohibited
ii) Manoeuvring load factor limits + 4.5g/0.0g
iii) In turbulent conditions do not exceed 250 kt IAS

The pilots notes must also be amended to show the above limitations. These limitations must be observed until further notice and may be revised when the CAA has completed its investigations." Enquiries regarding this LTO should be referred to Mr A C Love, General Aviation Section on 0293 573726.

CLINTON DECLARES VICTORY OVER FAA

No, not the President of the United States, but (in many peoples eyes) the real hero of the day Dave Clinton, who, after much hard work against the FAA after their attempt at the over-regulation of the warbirds scene in the United States recently declared *Victory* in an article in *Texans & Trojans* (the magazine of the *North American Trainer Association*). Sadly, *Warbirds Worldwide* cannot take any credit for the results of over 3000 letters written to the U.S. Federal Aviation Administration, though Editor Paul Coggan did transmit a strong letter of protest, and no doubt several hundred of our readers did lodge a complaint as well. Suffice to say the FAA did not respond, probably because they did not believe it was any of my (as a Brit)business. The credit must go to Dave Clinton for getting off his backside and actually doing something about the situation, and motivating others to do the same thing. Additionally of course the *Experimental Aircraft Association* and especially Bob Warner deserves full credit for overturning the FAA's intention to effectively ground the warbird fleet. It seems that the pen is mightier than the FAA's often wielded baseball bat. It also appears that some local FAA inspectors in various areas of the U.S.A. have been telling T-28 operators "Enjoy them while you can, we're going to stop your flying...." Let's hope that this abuse of power makes them choke on their words (and lose their jobs), and that such poor behaviour does not spread to the U.K., or any other part of the warbirds scene for that matter. It does however, seem that the heat is off, and we will be reporting on this in greater depth once things have settled down a little - in Journal 30. Meantime, Mr.David Clinton here's raising a glass or two to you - for I for one am pleased you have saved Warbirds operations from extinction. (Paul Coggan)

Let's Get'em Flying!

Industry News

Above: Columbia XJL-1 taking shape at Carlsbad - (Thierry Thomassin)

MARTIN AVIATION

The Columbia XJL-1 rebuild at Carlsbad has shown significant progress since our report in *Warbirds Worldwide 28*. The unique machine, with *Martin Aviation*, has seen the addition of floats, cowlings and wheel parts. Also at the same location Gnat N19GT has taken to the air for the first time.

PIONEER AERO

At *Pioneer Aero* the company is working on the rebuild of Elmer Ward's P-51D *Man O'War* - the wings were being cleaned outside during March and in the workshops another TF-51D is being built up for Michigan based Paul Peters. The port wing has been built by Art Teeters and his crew at *Cal Pacific Airmotive* and the starboard in house at *Pioneer*. The rebuild of the TF-51D is expected to be complete for the aircraft to attend Oshkosh 1994 this summer.

Pioneer is very much a long term business venture; the company have extensive spares holdings and tooling has been made for all those parts that they do not hold in stock, so the TF-51D will not be the last Mustang to be rolled out of their facility.

PACIFIC FIGHTERS

At *Pacific Fighters* that the first flight of Jack Erickson's Douglas AD4N Skyraider Bu 126867 N4277N/ex G-BMFB took place last February and the aircraft has been painted in the colours of VMC-1 in Korea, 1953.

FIGHTER REBUILDERS

Restoration of Steve Hinton's F8F Bearcat is still progressing with lots of work being undertaken since last January. The wing structure is now complete and reskinning is being underway. Bob Pond's F7F Tigercat Bu 80412/N7628C is now progressing inside the main workshops and both engines have been fitted. First flight is expected at the end of 1994. Work on the Bell P-59 has come to a halt, awaiting delivery of the wings from another contractor.

Are you rebuilding warbirds? We want to hear from you so we can report rebuilding activities Worldwide. Please write to the Editor.

YANKS AIR MUSEUM

The *Yankee Air Corps* has now changed its name to the *Yanks Air Museum*. Located at Chino, the museum has recently rolled out the beautiful P-51A N90358/43-6274 in 107th Tactical Photo Recce unit colours. Under rebuild here with Dave Gallop and Ango Hoos is Republic P-47D 45-49346, ex Brazilian Air Force (FAB) and now registered N3152D which will be for sale or trade on completion. Bell P-63C N9009 has been sold to the *Weeks Air Museum*.

Below: With the Yanks Air Museum is ex FAB Republic Thunderbolt N3152D / 45-49346 which will be for sale or trade (T. Thomassin)

AERO TRADER

The *Cavanaugh Flight Museum's* B-25 combat veteran is progressing rapidly at Aero Trader; the main spar has been changed and the front fuselage has been mated to the wing centre section recently. In store awaiting rebuild is another of the ex *Military Aircraft Restoration Company's* Iraqi Furies and the centre section of an ex Indonesian Air Force Mustang, currently for sale.

NORTHROP FLYING WING

The *Planes of Fame* Northrop Flying Wing (see P3 *Warbirds Worldwide 28*) is undergoing ground testing and final checks before it takes to the air. In March the engines (Franklin XO-540's) were being ground run with Ron Hackworth at the controls. Problems with the port engine have necessitated its replacement with the spare engine and the aircraft has not been flown as we went to press in mid-May

Top Right: *John Muszala of Pacific Fighters, Chino, running the Jack Erickson Douglas AD4N 126867 N4277N/ex G-BMFB. UK based warbird fans may remember this aircraft was parked at North Weald for some time.*
Centre: *Yanks Air Museum P-51A N90358/43-6274 now in olive drab camouflage; our major report held over to the next edition.* **Below:** *The Northrop Flying Wing N9MB undergoing engine runs at Chino last March with Ron Hackworth at the controls. Since then engine problems have forced the team to decide to change one of the units. Testing and ground trials are continuing as we go to press with the first flight now within reach. (Thierry Thomassin Photographs).*

Industry News

BROOKS AVIATION

Tom Wilson reports that significant progress is being made on the restoration of several Curtiss P-40's at Brooks Aviation, in Douglas, Georgia. Several fuselages are jigged and work has also commenced on several mainplanes. Photographs (above and below) show the fuselages and wings being rebuilt. Aircraft at Brooks Aviation include P-40C Tomahawks AK255 (being rebuilt to static) and AK295, P-40Es 41-5709, 41-35927 and 41-36843.

The team at Brooks include John Degroot, Dave Callaghan and of course the dynamic Tom Wilson. Tom also advises us that the company has just put into production P-40 wing extrusions. AK255 is awaiting gun bay doors (currently being manufactured), and has had a windscreen installed. Anyone interested in the wing extrusions or with P-40 parts can contact Tom on 912 383 0289.

AIRFRAME ASSEMBLIES

Airframe Assemblies have recently completed the wings for the David Price/Craig Charleston Bf109E-1 W.Nr. 3579 (see *Warbirds Worldwide* 25). The fuselage blocks are now also complete - on the '109 the fuselage sections are stretch formed and the blocks are now available for this to be undertaken. This has meant a significant investment in time, research and materials but it ensures that the Bf109 is rebuilt in exactly the same way that Messerschmitt built the aircraft originally. The wings from Me109J G-BOML have recently been returned to Duxford and work continues on the wings of MH434 both for the *Old Flying Machine Company*. Additionally there are several sets of Hawker Hurricane wings ready for rebuild for the new company *Hawker Restorations* in Suffolk.

Work continues on the three Hawker biplanes for *Aero Vintage*. The manufacture of parts for the Mustang and Storch is also under way. This year alone *Airframe Assemblies* have done work for eight Spitfires including Mk XIV TZ138 for Tiger Destefani in California and the South African Spitfire Mk IX, in addition to cowlings and other items for Seafire PR503 now with *AMJET* in Minneapolis. A pair of Spitfire V wings await rebuild.

A.J.D. ENGINEERING & HAWKER RESTORATIONS

A.J.D. Engineering in Suffolk, known primarily for their high quality work on World War I and vintage racing aeroplanes recently announced the formation of a new company in partnership with Sir Tim Wallis of the *Alpine Fighter Collection*. As previously reported in *Warbirds Worldwide* several Hurricanes have been purchased recently and *Hawker Restorations* has been established primarily to rebuild three of the type. The first Hurricane, P3351, is being built for the *Alpine Fighter Collection* in conjunction with *Air New Zealand*.

Continued on Page 12

LATE NEWS........

CAA's A8-20 FINALISED

Late news just in as we go to press concerns the Civil Aviation Document A8-20, Approval to carry out maintenance on ex military aircraft over 2730kg (basically Spitfire upwards). A list of companies approved under this heading will appear in the next edition of the Journal. The document is now finalised and is being printed.

Operation of such aeroplanes comes under CAP637(currently an external draft consultation document)and the Civil Aviation Authority (SRG) have written to 140 registered warbird owners seeking their opinions. We hope to be able to reveal the contents of the documents and make our assessment of their implications to the warbirds industry in the United Kingdom.

U.S. END VIETNAMESE AIRCRAFT BAN

Top: An A-37 in Vietnam being loaded on angled cradles to fit into a container (Noel Vinson)

Noel Vinson of *Australian Aviation Facilities Pty.Ltd.*, is offering for sale several Cessna A-37B Dragonfly's following the U.S. Governments decision to end the ban on aircraft imported from Vietnam. Noel explains "I made three trips to Vietnam, the first in 1990, and two subsequent trips. On the first trip the selection was good and good to fair quality; this eroded on subsequent trips (see photos) e.g. the Northrop F-5s disappeared as did a Bearcat and the A-37s were picked over with some basket cases lying around with a few good examples remaining. I imported four complete A-37Bs and one incomplete aircraft including 12 canned engines and a number of engines for spare parts. There are three others in Australia, one currently flying owned by David Lowey, one about to fly (Michael De Silva) and one well advanced (Hugh Farra). The New Zealand aircraft has now flown. The most impacting thing on the pilots here is the amazing acceleration required steep climb on take off so as not to exceed gear Vne.

I saw a photo in the US where a heat seeking missile buried itself into the left hand engine taking a large piece out of the fuse but the aircraft returned to base. I believe the A-37 is the safest jet warbird available today and I am sure statistics will back this up".

Above: Noel Vinson in front of a Northrop F5 67-2153, no longer there.

AERO-TECH AVIATION

SUPPLIER OF AN-MS-NAS
AIRCRAFT FASTENERS
FOR WARBIRDS WORLD WIDE

Proud Supplier to the restoration community including;

- CONFEDERATE AIR FORCE
- SANDERS AIRCRAFT
- PIONEER AIRCRAFT
- KAL AERO
- SAN DIEGO AERO MUSEUM
- PACIFIC FIGHTERS
- EZELL AVIATION
- Q G AVIATION
- BILL SPEER (PEGASUS)
- YOUNGS AIRFRAME

UK, European & Middle East Distributor for
AERO-TECH AVIATION USA
IS
AEROSPACE SUPPORT LTD

4 LYNEHAM ROAD
BICESTER
OXON OX6 7FD ENGLAND
Tel: 0869 246712
Fax 0869 323702

WE WELCOME PHONE AND FAX
ENQUIRIES FOR QUOTATIONS
AND PRICE/DELIVERY
PLEASE WRITE OR CALL FOR A
FREE CATALOGUE - LISTING
MOST COMMON ITEMS

**AERO-TECH AVIATION
1860B JOE CROSSON DR.
EL CAJON CA 92020 USA**
TEL: 1-800-448-4457   1-619-448-4485
FAX 619 448 7479

More Industry News overleaf

Industry News

This historic aircraft saw service in the Battle of France and the Battle of Britain before going to the USSR. Hurricane specialist Paul Mercer has recently joined the company. *Hawker Restorations* are investing heavily to ensure that the rebuilds are as original and authentic as possible, ensuring as much of the original structure as possible is utilised in the rebuild. This includes ensuring that all newly manufactured extrusions and other parts are matched exactly to the original specification. As related earlier the first aircraft is for The Alpine Fighter Collection and two Hurricanes will be put up for sale on completion. There are also other exciting developments in prospect and we will report on these in the next edition.

HISTORIC FLYING

At Audley End the number of aircraft on rebuild has increased over the past few months. The *Flying Legend* North American P-51D F-AZIE continues to make progress after being stripped to repair accident damage, alongside two Spitfire Mk V's, BM597, now with the *Historic Aircraft Collection* and another Mk V. plus a Mk. XIV for a British operator.

Significant work is also being undertaken on Spitfire Mk XVIII SM854/G-BUOS - the fuselage is currently jigged and is being reskinned.

The *Historic Aircraft Collection's* rare Yakovlev Yak-1, which has raised considerable interest since our report in *Warbirds Worldwide 24* continues to make progress but at a slower pace.

BAC JET PROVOST NEWS

The British Aircraft Corporation couldn't possibly have known that once their BAC Jet Provost and Strikemasters came to the end of their military careers they would quickly be snapped up by warbird jet operators and sport jet pilots.

The ex Singaporean Air Force Strikemasters now form the basis for the operation being run by *AMJET Services International* of St. Paul, Minnesota (Tel (612) 786 3818 - Fax (612) 786 1539). Vice President Bob Monahan reports that the 2nd February 1994 saw AMJET receive an airworthiness certificate from the FAA for BAC 167 N167SM. This is an ex Singapore aircraft (No.322) which was one of the eleven purchased from Steve Ferris at *International Air Parts* in Australia. AMJET also purchased all the ground support equipment and a huge inventory of parts. Back up support on this scale, reports Bob Monahan "....made it relatively easy to complete an 18 month total restoration on the aircraft, and it also proved to be very beneficial to other Strikemaster and Jet Provost owners here in the U.S.A." In the U.K. the Ministry of Defence surplussed the vast majority of all BAC Jet Provosts, formerly the mainstay of jet training in the Royal Air Force.

Some 67 airframes have been purchased by *Global Aviation* (Tel: 0472 251230, fax 0472-251450) of Grimsby, South Humberside. Of these Jet Provost Mk5A XW369 is currently flying with Lance Toland (see article on page 58) at Griffin, Georgia, and XW368, XW354, XW359, and XW415, are with Wiley Sanders at Troy, Alabama. Jet Provosts are being delivered to the former RAF airfield at Binbrook as we go to press. Several Strikemasters saw combat in minor skirmishes and the Jet Provost has seen many warbird pilots jet qualified over the years! **More Jet Reports on page 18**

BOOMERANG AVAILABLE

Matthew Denning reports from Queensland - The second pair of Boomerang wings have just come out of the jig. These are for Greg Batts CA-12 A46-54 and more are to follow.

Matthew has recently acquired more Boomerang fuselage frames and components from Darling Downs and reports he is now in the position of being able to build up a complete airworthy Boomerang to original specifications. The price to complete the second aircraft is $390,000 U.S. over an estimated period of two years. Matthew reports he has enough parts to build up just one more aircraft, so if anyone is serious about obtaining an example of this rare, unique Australian fighter this will probably be their only chance (readers may like to refer to *Warbirds Worldwide 24* and the major feature on the type as well as the update in *Warbirds Worldwide 28* - Ed).

Readers should also note that there is a video being produced entitled *The Boomerang Story* by *Nomad Productions* (see Page 42) which will show Guido Zuccoli's aircraft being put through its paces as well as footage of Greg Batts and Matthew Dennings' aircraft under rebuild - including wing construction.

Let's Get'em Flying!

GENERAL NEWS BRIEFING

Eddie Coventry of Earls Colne has another Yakovlev C.11 on rebuild with Phil Parrish. Appropriately registered G-IYAK it will join the already airworthy G-OYAK. Still in the U.K. Mark Jeffries of *Yak UK* has flown his Yak 11 172623/G-BTUB (ex EAF 543) on Friday 13th May from its base at Little Gransden.

The *Fighter Collection* have recently acquired a Japanese Nakajima Ki-43 Hayabusa (Oscar) from the *Australian War Memorial* - the aircraft arrived at Duxford in April and is the first Japanese warbird to arrive in the U.K. for restoration to flying condition. Arriving at the same base in May was Yakovlev Yak 11 F-AZOK/172503.

During January the well known P-51D Mustang N1051S was dispatched to a customer in the United States. Spencer Flack flew the aircraft extensively when it was based in the U.K.

After temporarily being painted as an Fw190 for the *Sky TV* mini series *Fall from Grace* (due to go out in June) the *Old Flying Machine Company's* Hawker Fury has been painted in its original and authentic Iraqi Air Force markings. G-BTTA was recovered from Iraq in the late '70's by Ed Jurist and David Tallichet. We hope to have an illustrated report on this aircraft in the next edition of the Journal.

The planned U.S. based warbird armada to Europe is looking unlikely as we go to press. It seems that several of the companies planning to sponsor the *Yankee Air Museum's* flight to Europe for the D-Day commemorative events have withdrawn their sponsorship at the last minute, though there is still a possibility that a small number of aircraft will make it.

Below: *From Tom Smith in Florida comes this shot of Supermarine Spitfire Mk XVI SL542 formerly an RAF gate guard, now with Mike Araldi in Lakeland, Florida where it will be rebuilt to flying condition. The Spitfire was used as a gate guard at RAF Horsham St. Faith in May 1957 then went to RAF Coltishall and finally to RAF St. Athan in Wales for disposal in 1989*

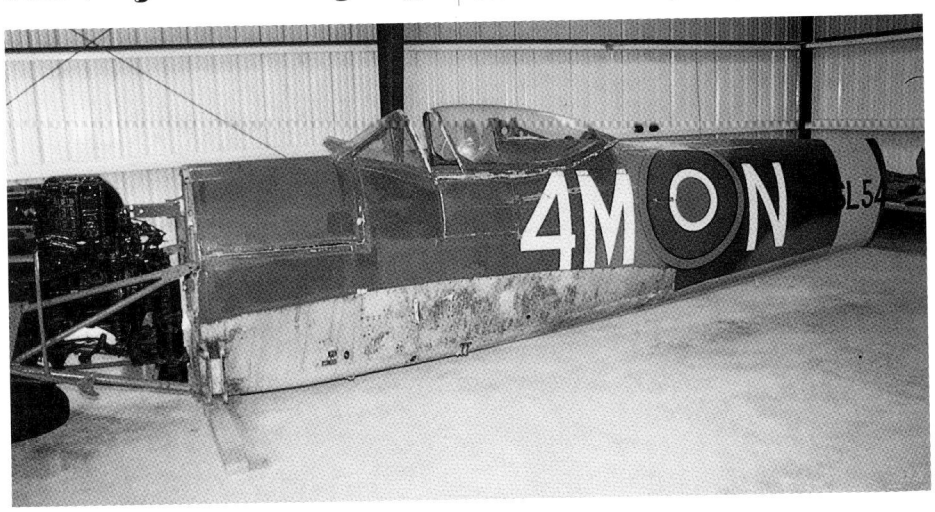

HISTORIC FLYING LIMITED
FOR REBUILDS

We have rebuilt a number of vintage and warbird aircraft to concours standard for several UK and overseas customers, and are currently involved in a number of projects. A team of experienced, skilled engineers able to tackle the challenges of working to the strictest modern safety standards whilst preserving the historical flavour of the original aircraft are ready to do work for you. £18.50 per hour

FOR FABRIC & PAINTING

Fabric Covering to traditional methods using 8F1 Irish Linen or modern equivalent ie Ceconite, Dacron, Stits or Razorback to customers personal specifications. Painting - from components through to complete aircraft - authentic finish if required. £17.50 per hour.

Historic Flying Limited,
The Mitchell Hangar, Audley End Airfield, Saffron Walden,
Essex CB11 4JG UK
Contact Mr. Tim Routsis

FOR MAINTENANCE

At Historic Flying we have all the facilities available to perform overhauls and routine maintenance, major annual checks, engine changes and to troubleshoot any problems you may have quickly and efficiently. We perform these tasks on any vintage aircraft or warbird, all to C.A.A. approvals. We are M3 approved (number AMR 358). Rates £20.00 per hour.

Tel: 0799 528084 or Fax 0799 524699 for immediate personal attention.

VINTAGE V-12'S, INC.
Specializing in World War II Aircraft Engines

Overhauls, Parts and Worldwide Service For:

- MERLINS
- ALLISONS
- GRIFFONS
- DB 601
- DB 605
- BRISTOL CENTAURUS

Buyers of Engines, Parts, Tools and Manuals of the Above Listed Engines.

In Europe Contact
Craig Charleston
FAX 44-206-240450

OFFERING OVER 20 YEARS EXPERIENCE

Mike Nixon, President
P.O. Box 920
1582 East Goodrick Rd.
Tehachapi, CA 93581
United States
(805) 822-3112
FAX (805) 822-3120

"*Quality Engines for Quality People.*"

Curtiss Wright / Pratt & Whitney

**Parts & Service
(904) 578-2800**

AIMS SHIPPING & FORWARDING LTD

Experienced Specialists in the import and export of civil and military aircraft. We offer Container-Conventional-Roll On/Roll Off Service World Wide at very competitive rates. Our Service Includes:

SURVEYS - PROJECTS - INSURANCE - DOCUMENTATION - DISMANTLING - PACKING AND SECURING INTERNATIONAL AND DOMESTIC HAULAGE

We also have our own in house sourcing department for aircraft and parts in Eastern Bloc and Third World countries. It costs little to contact us by telephone or fax for a competitive quotation tailored to suit your needs

Tel: 0708 860139/861516   Fax 0708 861497

Rain Hits Shuttleworth

One of the world's most famous collections of unique, historic, airworthy aircraft is having to take a hard look at its profitability this year. *The Shuttleworth Collection* are not operating in the black, due, in part, to a particularly wet season in 1993. At a Press Briefing on May 1st, 1994, Sir John Charnley, Chairman of the Trustees outlined the situation as faced by the Executive Committee.

After the 1993 season, the 'Collection need to make savings of £50,000 in the 1994/5 period. This can be set against an expected capital expenditure of £250,000 over the next five years. The 1993 season was unfortunate in that a significant number of shows were washed out or rained on and *Shuttleworth* is currently 90% dependent on revenue from the airshows put on through the summer. Though a charitable foundation, the *Shuttleworth* still has to break even each year. Old Warden is not able to expand in size and part of *Shuttleworth's* charm is its apparently unchanging nature. The aim for the future is nevertheless to endeavour to widen the appeal for a family day out throughout the year. Professional advice is being taken to improve presentation, evaluate the popularity of the individual exhibits and to utilise the site for corporate events. Given that the amount of money

Above: *One of Shuttleworth's key exhibits - Gloster Gladiator G-AMRK on 2nd May 1994 (James Kightly)*

spent currently on staffing and resources is as lean and competitive as possible (though the expenditure outlay is roughly even throughout the year) it is another intention of the Collection's Trustees to offer for sale some of the less popular vehicles and aircraft in the *Shuttleworth Collection*.

The future does not look easy for the them, but they have hopefully taken all the necessary steps to ensure that they survive. Don't just wish them luck, patronise their airshows!
WW James Kightly

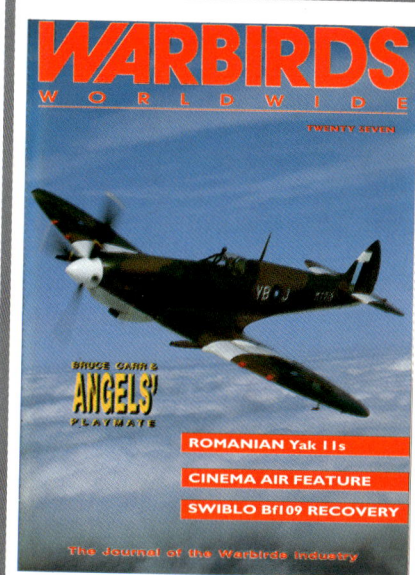

Warbirds Worldwide is available on subscription: UK £18.50, REST OF EUROPE £21.00- USA $44.00, Canada $C48.00, Australia $A49.00, New Zealand NZ$59.00 Hong Kong £24.00. Asia £24.00 We accept VISA, MASTERCARD, and AMEX or you can pay by personal cheque in local currency. For Europe Eurocheques are preferred. Please send fee to the address below (Please note we have an office in North America) or Fax credit card details to (0623)845556 telling us which copy you wish to start with. All publications are sent by *Air Mail* in card envelopes.

Get it First Get it Fast - subscribe today!

Subscribe Today!

Warbirds Worldwide P.O. Box 99., Mansfield, Notts NG19 9GU, ENGLAND
North American Office: Midwest Aviation Museum
RR6 Box 325 Danville IL 61832 USA

PREVIEW Flying Legends Air Show 16th & 17th July 1994

The Fighter Collection is organising, for the Imperial War Museum at Duxford, a show which will hopefully be a worthy successor to the former *Classic Fighter* Air Display, which has been much mourned by warbirds enthusiasts if the number of calls to the *Warbirds Worldwide* offices is anything to go by.

After a trial one day event last year, which according to the organisers, was an immense success, *Flying Legends Air Show* has now moved to the premier July spot. For two days on the 16th and 17th, when the skies in the Cambridge area will roar with the sounds of millions of pounds worth of historic hardware.

The *Fighter Collection* could run an impressive air show on the basis of their own stable of flyable fighter aircraft but have booked outstanding aircraft of the *Shuttleworth Collection, Old Flying Machine Company, Duke Of Brabant Air Force, Sabena Old Timers, Battle of Britain Memorial Flight, Jean Salis Collection, Flying Legend Organisation, Tante Ju52, B-17 Preservation, Plane Sailing, Scandinavian Historic Flight*, together with British Aerospace Mosquito, South African Air Force and many others, including numerous private *legends* owners aircraft.

Not only have a large number of the scheduled participants never been seen before in the U.K. there are two major initiatives being planned which will no doubt appeal to many of our readers. This includes a special opportunity during the morning for photographers to go "live side", for those very special shots of the 40+ aircraft participating - and with *The Fighter Collection's* P-38, Wildcat and Skyraider in new livery and the unique foreign participants, Fuji and Kodak should have a most profitable day!

Another first for Duxford is a special *Legends Gold Pass* which, when purchased in advance, is transferable on both days and enables entry to an exclusive V.I.P. tented area and prime view enclosure. Availability of a first class lunch, tea or licensed bar will make this a popular place to entertain guests or mingle with the many famous past and present pilots who will be attending.

The stars of *Flying Legends* are almost too numerous to mention but will include the first appearance in Britain of the Griffon powered South African Air Force Shackleton, the Sabena *Old Timers* Lysander, four Mustangs not seen in the UK before (on top of the resident UK contingent) as well as the favourites, Lancaster, B-17, Mosquito, three B-25 Mitchells, the elegant Hawker Hind and historic Bristol Fighter, and the BMW engined Junkers Ju52. The Grumman trio of Wildcat, Hellcat, Bearcat, will all be demonstrated alongside the Bf109G *Black 6*, the immortal Gloster Gladiator, Tony le Vier's *Cosmic Wind* and the beautiful P-38 Lightning (now in 20th Fighter Group olive drab paint scheme). A pair of Hawker Hurricanes plus Spitfires from Mk's II to XIX will complete the assembly and flying of over *Forty* legendary aircraft. They will be airborne in various scenarios and formations, being flown from this historic venue in a very historic year. It is now over a decade since *The Fighter Collection* was formed and they have become famous all over Europe for their warbird demonstrations.

Warbirds Worldwide's readership is the serious historian and warbird aircraft "aficionado".In the words of Stephen Grey, "...*The Flying Legends Airshow* is tailor made for them ....no helicopters, no Pitts, no parachutists, no dogs and ponies". We are convinced it will become the international historic airshow event of the calendar, pulling together the European warbird population

The FLYING LEGENDS Airshow

Left: *The aircraft that started it all - P-51D Moose with WW Chief Pilot Mark Hanna of The Old Flying Machine Company at the controls. Above: Spitfire ML417 in formation with the newly painted Wildcat in Fleet Air Arm colours. Below: The Wildcat on its own: FM-2 N4845V/Bu86711 was formerly with Eric Mingledorf of LA and was on display at the Chennault Aviation Museum before being acquired for the Fighter Collection - all photographs from Fighter Collection Photographer John Dibbs. Copyright Fighter Collection/John Dibbs.*

WARBIRDS WORLDWIDE will be attending the Flying Legends Airshow both days
Come and see us, meet the Editor and
some of our contributors on STAND 48

Industry News continued from page 12

JET REPORT USA

At Chino, *Paradise Aero*, a new company, have recently imported ten ex French Air Force Fouga Magister jets. The company, run by Steve Sutherland, has at least three of the aircraft at Chino including N395F/No.395

Further afield in Texas *Sierra Hotel* at Addison continue to expand with several new aircraft and a continuing restoration programme on others. The large, classic Vietnam era shape of the Thud (Republic F-105 Thunderchief 630343) now dominates the *SH* apron at Addison (shown Right - Thierry Thomassin photo) and makes an interesting partner for F-104 60780 which belongs to a private individual (shown below). Also at this location being rebuilt for the *Cavanaugh Flight Museum* is a MiG-15UTI and MiG-21UTI (ex Polish Air Force). As we were going to press news also came in of the delivery of an ex Canadian Armed Forces F-101 Voodoo which is scheduled to become the last airworthy Voodoo in the world.

JET REPORT UK

Under the personal guidance of His Majesty King Hussein of the Hashemite Kingdom of Jordan, the Royal Jordanian Air Force (*RJAF*) has formed a *Historic Flight*. The unique flight will reflect the RJAF's distinguished heritage of the past four decades. It will, for the immediate future, be based in the U.K. The *RJAF Historic Flight*, the world's only national all jet historic flight, will initially operate the first two types of jet fighter with which it was equipped in the 1950's - the de Havilland Vampire and the Hawker Hunter. Representative two-seat versions of these aircraft, a Vampire T.55 and a Hunter T.7 have been acquired on behalf of the *RJAFHF*.

The Vampire T55 represents the first jet aircraft to be flown by the RJAF. It became operational almost 40 years ago and then comprised ten Vampire FB.9s and three Vampire T.11s donated by the Royal Air Force. Following the tragic loss of a similar aircraft that had been flown by the RAF's *Vintage Pair*, the Vampire T.55, a former Swiss Air Force aircraft (U-1216/ZH563/G-BVLM), was presented to the *RAF Benevolent Fund* in 1990.

It had originally been hoped that the Swiss Vampire could be kept airworthy by the R.A.F. as a replacement. However, this did not prove possible and now the aircraft will fly in the colours of the Royal Jordanian Air Force.

The Hunter T.7 (G-BOOM shown right by Peter R. March) has been painted in an appropriate camouflage scheme to represent the first of twelve ex-RAF Hunter F6s delivered to the RJAF in 1958. It carries the markings of No. 1 Fighter Squadron (RJAF) that was based at Mafraq. The RJAF received a trio of two-seat Hunter T66Bs in 1960. All of the surviving Hunters were retired in 1974 and handed over to the Sultanate of Oman as a gift the following year.

It is hoped to locate a suitable single-seat Vampire and Hunter to add to the Flight in due course. Other types can be expected in the future from the current fleet of *RJAF* jet fighters (Northrop F-5A/B, F-5E/F Tiger and Mirage F.1) as they in turn become historic aircraft. Several former RJAF F-104A Starfighters have already been retained with one being restored to taxiable condition. The F-104 could be a candidate for the Flight at some time in the future.

Jet Heritage at Bournemouth has been retained to prepare, maintain and display the *RJAF Historic Flight's* aircraft whilst they are in the U.K. A limited number of flying display appearances will be made in 1994 and will include the RAF Benevolent Fund's *International Air Tattoo* at RAF Fairford on 30-31 July, an event long supported by King Hussein and the RJAF. Further information and contact with the *RJAF Historic Flight* can be made through Richard Verrall (by fax only) on 0734 402275. Report from Peter R. March.

Still with *Jet Heritage*, Hawker Hunter F4 XE677/G-HUNN took to the air for its first post restoration test flight last January. The ex 111 Squadron RAF Hunter ended its operational days at Loughborough University as an instructional airframe before being rescued and rebuilt by *Jet Heritage*. It will appear in a stunning overall black paint scheme as used by the official RAF aerobatic team the *Black Arrows* in the 1950's. To book the aircraft for displays contact Adrian Gjertsen on 0202 581 676 or Fax 0202 581 675 (Gary Brown report).

Let's Get'em Flying!

Victoria AIR MAINTENANCE

David Maude updates us on recent activities at Victoria Air Maintenance, Sidney, BC.

Above: David Clinton of Darton International has his T-28 N280DC in at VAM for reskinning of wing leading edges and a full strip and paint.

1994 will undoubtedly be another banner year at Russ Popel's Victoria Air Maintenance. Currently there are no less than seven T-28's, two DH Otters, a Hawker Sea Fury and a Yak 18 in the hangar.

1993 was the busiest in the company's history, with several T-28s, O-2 and Yak 18 restorations, and the completion of Dr. Rich Sugden's T-2 'Buckeye' (Bu 155226, registration N212TB). As well as routine maintenance on numerous warbirds. The Buckeye was a special project consisting of a signature VAM 'ground-up' rebuilding of this unique jet. As the T-2 is still an active U.S. Military aircraft, parts location was particularly difficult - it seems the spares are well guarded U.S. military property, resulting in endless scrounging of parts from scrap yards, collectors and military suppliers. The end result was an outstanding aircraft, the only T-2B flying in civilian hands, and a restoration that both owner and restorer can be proud of. *Warbirds Worldwide* will report on this in depth in the next edition.

A long time speciality, North American T-28's continue to dominate the workload at VAM. Several projects are slated to become airborne this year, including Ak Ftaya's T-28C model. A good deal of the work on this project is being undertaken by Ak personally, including the paint stripping...this is a true warbird lover! Dave Clinton's Trojan N280DC is in for a full strip and paint, as well as having the leading edges reskinned. The VAM 'company car' T-28C- currently perhaps the ugliest T-28 in the air, sporting a 'fresh from Tucson' look, it too will some day have it's turn in the restoration shop.

Don Crowe's Sea Fury N60SF *Simply Magnificent* is in the hangar after hatching its engine at Reno in 1993. The aircraft was disassembled and trucked to

Below; Dr. Rich Sugden's North American T-2B Buckeye which was rebuilt at VAM. Because the aircraft is still on active military service it was very difficult to get parts for it. Seen here with 'everything hanging'. (Grant Hopkins)

Industry News - Victoria Air Maintenance

Victoria, where it awaits it's new Centaurus from Mike Nixon's *Vintage V-12's*. Before being reassembled, some sheet metal work was done on the wing centre section. Don looks forward to returning to the race circuit in 1994. A full history of VAM was contained in *Warbirds Worldwide* 15, and the company continues to operate a fully equipped warbird restoration shop, including paint and sheet metal facilities for aircraft from L-4's to Albatross and beyond. Members wishing further information on shop availability are requested to contact: Russ Popel, President, Victoria Air Maintenance, 9550 Canora Road, Sidney, BC, CANADA, V8L 4Rl. Phone: (604) 656-7600

WARBIRDS
W O R L D W I D E

Don Crowe's Sea Fury N60SF awaiting Centaurus engine from Mike Nixon's Vintage V-12s.

Few warbird aficionados will fail to agree that the Messerschmitt Me-262 *Schwalbe* was the world's first truly operational jet fighter and nearly rewrote world aviation history by being so far ahead of its time. Unfortunately today, the few that still exist are cloistered in museums, never to fly again as originally built due to airframe corrosion and non-availability of operative original *Jumo 004* engines. Ask many enthusiasts which warbird they would like to see fly again given a free hand and a high percentage will answer 'Me-262'. Despite a growing warbird jet movement worldwide some die hard piston enthusiasts will *not* accept later jets as warbirds, yet the '262 has massive appeal.

The Messerschmitt Me-262 programme is being conducted jointly by *Classic Fighter Industries* and the *Texas Airplane Factory*. An operational Messerschmitt Me-262 is considered to be the Holy Grail of aircraft by many collectors - passionately desired, but unattainable; regarded by many as 'mission impossible'. Now four new Messerschmitts Me-262's are being built, each one described 'as genuine an original as those that flowed from Messerschmitt's war-time production lines'.

Historically, the Me-262 has been recognised as one of the most beautiful aircraft of all time. Looked upon by many as a perfect expression of form following function.

The hard facts of war forced Messerschmitt engineers to surpass all their previous efforts to create a simple, sturdy airframe able to withstand the rigours of high speed combat. They did not know that they were also blazing the way for the North American F-86 and the Boeing B-47, both of which used the Messerschmitt swept-wing experience to dominate the cold war.

The operational career of the twin-jet *Schwalbe* (Swallow) was a fitting complement to its beauty and performance. It was brought into battle at a time when the proud German

Above: *The jigs containing the first Me262 fuselage at Texas Airplane Company (CFI)*

Luftwaffe was tormented by premier fighter aircraft in the world. Veteran German aces like Adolf Galland and Johannes Steinhoff felt themselves lucky to fly the new jet fighter, calling it "life insurance" while Jimmy Doolittle and Tooey Spaatz instantly recognised it as a threat to the Eighth Air Force's hard won air superiority. Steve Snyder of *CFI* comments "The Me-262 was revolutionary in concept, execution and employment then; I am sure it will be just as revolutionary today In offering our present and future generations the unique opportunity to actually see this superb aircraft in flight".

Time has not treated the existing Me-262

Texas 262's

Following their extremely successful venture building Grumman F3F's Classic Fighter Industries and The Texas Airplane Factory are now building Messerschmitt Me262s population well. Of the total production, only nine airframes are known to exist, all of them in museums and none of them even close to being airworthy. One of the few original Me-262 aircraft in existence is currently residing with *Classic Fighter Industries* and is being used as the reference point for the reverse engineering effort. The availability of this aircraft (Nr.110639) from NAS Willow Grove has made the entire project both possible and practical. A careful study of the original blueprints, along with continual cross-referencing to an existing aircraft have allowed the '262 Project team to unveil and duplicate every one of the *Schwalbe's* structural secrets.

For the first time in history, *Classic Fighter Industries* has brought together a remarkable confluence of imagination, engineering data, rare aircraft parts and a master craftsman's manufacturing skill to present a unique opportunity to produce operational Messerschmitt Me-262s.

Flying this ultimate classic now becomes a reality, following a path blazed not only by Luftwaffe greats, but also by famous American and English test pilots like Hal Watson, Russ Schleeh, Al Boyd and Eric Brown, all of whom had the highest praise for the flight handling qualities of the *Schwalbe*.

Owners have a choice of selecting the single-seat Me-262A-1A or the twin seat B-1A with an optional conversion kit that can adapt it to single seat configuration in about four hours.

How does Charles think the new production aircraft will be viewed by collectors? "Please let me re-emphasise that these aircraft will be identical in every respect to the production planes that came off the Messerschmitt line in Germany. The aircraft will be fabricated exactly "as it was" during the conflict, with exact attention to every detail, including every minor item like hydraulic fittings, electrical connections and all mechanical elements". And how have the aircraft been adapted to fit the airworthiness and safety requirements of the 1990's?

Charles again "It is well known that the original Jumo-004 axial flow-engines were unreliable because they were brought into production far too early in their development cycle. These powerplants did not enjoy the advantages of high temperature metal alloy construction and were only rated for an average life of twenty hours or less. Therefore, in the interest of safety this program has adopted the use of the very reliable General Electric J-85 jet engines (basically the Lear jet engine) as the propulsion source".

In fact, *Classic Fighter Industries* has put together a unique solution to the propulsion aspect of the '262 project. By integrating the much smaller J-85 engine into a hollow mock up external aluminium casting shell of the Jumo-004, the combined mass and weight properties of the original engines are preserved which in turn assures that the original wing

Above: The two seat Me262 fuselage. Owners have a choice of selecting the single-seat Me-262A-1A or the twin seat B-1A with an optional conversion kit that can adapt it to single seat configuration in about four hours. According to a report received from Classic Fighter Industries in late April four aircraft only will be produced including the two seater aircraft (CFI)

bending stresses and flutter margins of the original 262 are retained. Most appropriately for a project of this nature, is the fact that the appearance of the Jumo 004 engine is accurately displayed when the nacelle cowlings are opened!

Steve Snyder added "Classic Fighter Industries has provided for the installation of powerful disc brakes within the drum housings found on the original aircraft. Significant improvement in stopping distances are achieved with no visible change to the external appearance of the wheel assembly". Both Steve Snyder and Charles Searock agree that the heart of the project is the technical skill of a true 'national treasure' in aircraft construction, mastercraftsman Herb Tischler. Tischler, whose fifty years of experience building aircraft began in the *Henschel Flugzeugwerke* aviation school in 1941, has distinguished himself with a series of beautiful aircraft construction projects culminating most recently in four remarkable Grumman F3F biplanes now active and flyable.

Tischler is using the only existing Messerschmitt Me-262 B-1A; (dual control aircraft) as a pattern to create new production parts. Every element of the aircraft's structure is being duplicated with original materials, using metric measurements. Because the original Me-262 design team was driven by a quest for simplicity as well as performance for combat use, a new production *Schwalbe* delivers executive jet speed and altitude capability with minimum maintenance requirements. Charles is keen to point out "This airplane is not a "systems" aircraft. There is no hydraulic type control system, only simple direct mechanical linkages, without even hydraulic boost. The electrical system is extremely simple but the new aircraft will be provided with a complete self starting capability so that any small airport with a 3500ft. runway can be con-

veniently utilised".

The complete cockpit instrumentation and details are laid out exactly as they were originally. Modern avionics and radios may be concealed under removable consoles or mock instrument faces at the buyer's option.

Along with voluminous data, the project team has obtained five complete sets of original instruments, rudder pedals, control sticks and other functional elements. One notable acquisition is an original FUG 220 Lichenstein intercept radar, available if the two seat B1-A radar night fighter version is desired.

The run of four new production Messerschmitt Me-262s will not be extended unless all owners of the first four agree to an extension, and jointly establish a price for an "extra" aircraft.

Each customer is being kept fully informed by monthly progress reports on each individual aircraft, including video cassette and pictures. Construction of the complete airframes is planned to take from 36 to 42 months and the project is already on schedule, 10 months into production.

"The potential of the Messerschmitt Me-262 aircraft...." says Charles Searock ..."for exhibition, airshows and film work is as unlimited as its potential for pure flying pleasure". With the emergence of the Grumman F3Fs from the same organisations last year the critics were silenced. Both *Classic Fighter Industries* and *Texas Airplane Factory* have an admirable track record and we look forward to future updates on this exciting project in future editions of *Warbirds Worldwide*.

DUTCH MUSTANG FLIGHT ASSOCIATION
DAMN YANKEE COMES TO HOLLAND

P-51D

On Wednesday the 6th April, a North American P-51D arrived at Lelystad Airport. The aircraft, which was packed inside a huge sea container was placed in front of the *Aero Service B.V.* hangar. The container was shipped from Los Angeles to the port of Rotterdam, and trucked to Lelystad Airport. The P-51D was moved out of the dark container, and work started immediately to put the Mustang back together. With the assistance of the previous owner, Bill Klaers of Klaers Aviation, the job was done in just two days. On the 8th April, Bill made a successful test flight.

This P-51D-30NA, registered N11T (44-74425) belongs to *Western Maintenance Inc.* a company based at Mesa, Arizona. This beautiful Mustang was brought to Holland by Mr. Tom van der Meulen. A deal was struck with the owners, to base the P-51 in Holland and exploit it on a neutral budget, for *Western Maintenance Inc.* The Mustang will fly through a newly formed organisation called: *P-51 Dutch Mustang Flight Association*, based at Lelystad Airport. Tom van der Meulen is president of *Aero Service B.V.* His company employs about 10 people operating some 18 aircraft. His main business is agricultural flying and aircraft rental. He also keeps a Fairchild F24 and Boeing PT-17 Stearman in one of his hangars. The company started operating back in 1958 and through the years Tom made many friends and contacts, especially in the U.S. After being offered several vintage aircraft in the United States during business trips the idea formed to bring a warbird to Holland. No suitable aircraft was found... until he noted the Packard-engined North American P-51 Mustang, N11T in Arizona. Through the business contact with *W.M. Inc.* Tom was able to come to an arrangement to bring the Mustang to Holland. During February this year the final contracts where sorted out and the Mustang was transported to L.A.

44-74425 has no combat experience, having delivered (on the 28th May 1945), from the N.A.A. Inglewood plant. With c/n 122-40965 to charge number NA.122, she is from the 10th production batch of P-51D s serials 44-74227 to 44-75026 (under contract number AC-2378). On the 31st October 1945 she was based at the 302nd Base Unit, Continental Air Force, Hunter AFB in Georgia. On the 8th of November 1950 she was taken on strength by the RCAF, serving with No 403, *City of Calgary* Squadron (Northwest Air Command) serialed 9591. During December1959 '25 was placed on the American register as N6522D to Intercontinental Airways, Canasota, New York. In 1978 she was re-registered N11T.

According to Tom the Mustang arrived in Holland on time, in order to participate in the 1994 airshow season. The Mustang is painted in the colours of 356 Fighter Group, 359 Fighter Squadron 8th USAAF, based at Martlesham Heath, Suffolk, and carries the code OC-G. *Damn Yankee* is already booked for several airshows in Holland, Belgium, France and in England. She is also available for memorial flights and Liberation fly bys (D-Day) throughout the year. For the 1994 D-Day commemorations it is hoped N11T will fly with the Dutch Spitfire and the *Duke of Brabant* B-25 Mitchell. Tom van der Meulen will fly the Mustang during its stay in Europe. **WW Michael Prophet.**

Let's Get'em Flying!

Airframe Assemblies Ltd
Vintage Aircraft Sheet Metal Specialists

Parts manufactured include items for:
HURRICANE
SPITFIRE
TEMPEST
HUNTER
LIGHTNING
THUNDERBOLT
MESSERSCHMITT
SEAFIRE
HAWKER BI PLANES

Light aircraft work
also undertaken.
Any other sheet metal
requirements you may
have for other vintage aircraft
can be produced to drawing or pattern.

If you are contemplating an historic aircraft rebuild please contact:
Unit 4/5, Faulkner Road, Sandown,
Isle of Wight PO36 9AY
Tel: 0983 404462
Fax: 0983 402806

Complete rebuild of wings in jigs with new spars

— We have produced parts for piston and jet warbirds all over the world —

PRECISION AIRMOTIVE CORPORATION

Is it overhaul time for your Large Pratt & Whitney or Curtis Wright Radial Engine?

Come to the Leader in the Industry

Precision Airmotive has over 45 years experience in the overhaul and repair of Pratt & Whitney and Curtis Wright radial engines. For the most reliable overhaul in the aviation industry call or fax.

Phone (206) 353-8181
Fax: (206) 348-3545

FAA Repair Station HJ6R589N

T-28 FOR SALE

8500 hours TT, 125 hours since complete de-mate, re-wire and rebuild to "better than new". King Silver Crown, S-Tec autopilot, all Darton kits, O^2 system. low time "B" propeller, Halon fire system, full IFR with HSI, etc. Call for list of features and equipment
Bill Scully (310) 695-0511
UNITED STATES

The Anachronistic Swordfish

Looking like a refugee from the First World War, the Fairey Swordfish was obsolete before World War II began. Nothing about the Swordfish's story is mundane though, and as a deceptively harmless looking aircraft, this antique was able to change the course of World War II in almost every theatre of the war at sea, and it was responsible for sinking a greater tonnage of enemy shipping than any other allied aircraft. It is not our intention to tell the story of the *Stringbag* here: that has been done very well elsewhere, but a few facts about this uniquely British aircraft will serve to place this warbird in context.(The Swordfish's sobriquet of *Stringbag* has been given a number of different explanations; that a housewife on a shopping spree couldn't carry more items in her stringbag; the number of flying and landing wires that called the aircraft home made it look like a stringbag, etc. etc., Whatever the truth of it, the name always seemed to fit the aircraft!)

It is a big aircraft - standing 12 foot high, and requiring the crew to climb a huge white wall of canvas to reach their cockpit. On the face of it, it was a very unsophisticated machine ("and coming into land was there really nothing to remember, no cockpit drill at all?") and its reputation as a docile, manoeuvrable pilot's aeroplane was true. Nevertheless if you were ham-fisted enough it was still possible to strip the wings off the aircraft in a dive, or stall the machine; but you'd have to be really trying,

The Swordfish was used in World War II in many theatres simply because there was nothing else which was available, or better at dropping torpedoes, keeping submarines at bay or just capable of doing the job. Sometimes in a war the ability to fly slowly (top speed 138mph, less with a load) and to be exceptionally manoeuvrable can be a major advantage. One theory of Swordfish survival in wartime being that flak and fighters could not believe anything was flying that slowly in a battle, and they therefore fired their guns AHEAD of the aircraft! The Russians used the Polikarpov Po2 in a similar manner for nuisance raids on the Russian front; while the Communists used some decidedly odd types in Vietnam and Korea to fulfil similar roles.

In the same vein, the Douglas AD4 Skyraider was hardly the latest thing in aviation in the high-technology Vietnam war, but it didn't do so badly. While considering load carrying ability, look at what the Swordfish could manage using that 'extra' wing; (let's leave aside the derisory single fixed forward firing Vickers .303 and flexibly mounted Vickers K.303 machine gun) select from one 18 inch, 1610 lb torpedo, (the much more advanced 'modern' TBM Avenger could manage a 22 inch torpedo) a 1500 lb mine, eight rocket projectiles, a overload petrol tank, flares, dinghy pack, depth charges, and bombs of various descriptions up to 1500 lb total weight, Park the 'BAe' Swordfish at Farnborough, and array that lot in front of it, and it would leave several modern attack aircraft looking a lot less impressive!

WW James Kightly

Top: The film Sink the Bismarck utilised two airworthy Swordfish: LS326 and NF389 (see article entitled Stringbaggers on next page) credit: BFI Stills. Above: LS326 at Duxford in 1986. Both RNHF aircraft, though civil registered, are flown as Naval aircraft and as such the civil identity is Dormant (James Kightly).

SWORDFISH VARIANTS

Fairey Swordfish Mk.I with a 690 hp, Pegasus IIIM 9 cylinder radial engine,

Fairey Swordfish Mk.II with a 750 hp, Pegasus XXX engine (except early production examples which still has a Pegasus IIIM) and metal skinned lower wings to take rocket-projectiles.

Fairey Swordfish Mk.III equipped with a bulbous container between the undercarriage legs for the A.S.V. Mk.X radar: naturally it was known as a 'pregnant Stringbag'.

Fairey Swordfish Mk.IV: which was NOT an official designation but was often used to denote those Canadian airframes which were equipped with an enclosed cockpit canopy. Most of the Canadian survivors are Mk.II's, and all have been restored without the canopy, though originally equipped with it.

James Kightly introduces our major feature on the Stringbag with some background Swordfish facts

Let's Get'em Flying!

Swordfish Mk.II LS326

Old Faithful

The history of Fairey Swordfish LS326 is as varied and interesting as that of the type itself. Built by Blackburn at Sherburn-in-Elmet in 1943, it was known that LS326 had served during the war on communications and training being based at R.N.A.S. Culham near Oxford, and R.N.A.S. Worthy Down near Winchester, but until the 1980's details of her wartime use were still sketchy and it was not realised until then that LS326 was concealing a secret in her war service. In 1945 she was to be seen in company with a wide range of Allied and captured Axis aircraft at the victory parade in Hyde Park in London, but unlike most other parade aircraft she was to survive the lean post-war years through being one of six Swordfish acquired by Faireys in September 1945. Fairey's plan was apparently to convert the aircraft to crop sprayers but this did not come to fruition, and the five other aircraft were scrapped, LS326 being retained as a company hack, based at Heston. On May 28th, 1947 Faireys registered their Swordfish as G-AJVH, choosing the demob suiting of Fairey blue fuselage and silver flying surfaces. The new colours were applied at Hamble where the aircraft had been flown by Peter Twiss, the famous test pilot.

Put into store by Faireys at White Waltham, the aircraft suffered all the problems of such stored aircraft and was deteriorating rapidly due to the attentions of souvenir hunters and old age; one observer at the time commenting: "I felt a sense of severe shock at seeing the state of the components and later there was talk of rebuilding it once Fairey had fully transferred from Heston to White Waltham, but nothing happened until 1954 when the sad remains were taken back to Hamble once more by road."

Apparently Sir Richard Fairey had seen the Fleet Air Arm's beautiful silver Swordfish NF389 trundling around the sky at a Naval gathering, and remembering that his company had their own *Stringbag*, he gave instructions for the aircraft to be restored to airworthy condition. This was in 1954, and the aircraft needed a great deal of work to make it flyable.

Many parts had to be salvaged from scrap yards and naval dumps around the country, and without the existence of either a warbird movement or much of a vintage aircraft scene items such as flying wires were very hard to come by. The work was coordinated by Archie Pitt who had been charged with the job by Sir Richard, almost the whole of 1955 being required to complete the massive task. After the restoration had been completed by the dedicated workers at Hamble, LS326 flew again in October of that year, achieving a test flight 'best' of 127 kts at an all up weight of 7000lb in the hands of Geoffrey Allington.

In 1958 *20th Century Fox* asked Faireys if they could borrow the aircraft and use it in their forthcoming film *Sink the Bismarck*, It was repainted in a rather odd interpretation of 1941 colours, including the '5A' in post-war proportions, of Lt Cdr Eugene Esmonde. In company with the Royal Navy's Stringbag NF389, and with LS326 being flown by Peter Twiss, the two aircraft were filmed and recorded taking off and landing aboard *H.M.S. Centaur* for the film work (the penultimate occasion a Stringbag was to operate from a carrier), was well received, but the extensive model work required for the apparent destruction of the Bismarck, *H.M.S. Hood*, and the Swordfish aircraft, disguised the contribution of the two real aeroplanes.

It looked like LS326 was set for a pleasant career as a display aircraft, starting her 1959 appearances with a display at beautiful R.N.A.S. Lossiemouth on the Moray Firth for their Air Day, going on in that summer to appear at several other venues. Time was running out for Fairey Aviation however, and in mid-1960 they were absorbed into the Westland Group. Five months after the take-over, in September 1960, the now orphaned aircraft was donated to the Fleet Air Arm by Westlands. The Board of the Admiralty decided in their wisdom that the aircraft could go on flying '...so long as its condition remained good...after which it was to revert to static display '.

One beneficial result of this was that the Swordfish was to become the nucleus around which the *Royal Navy Historic Flight* (RNHF) was to be built, Sea Fury TF956 being received in airworthy condition from Hawker Aircraft in 1971, and Firefly AS.6 WB271 coming back from Australia in 1967 courtesy of a group of officers aboard *H.M.S. Victorious* (the machine flying again in 1972, when the Flight was formed), After formation other aircraft were taken on, including Sea Fury T20 WG655 and Hawker Sea Hawk FGA6 WV908 as well as Tiger Moths T8191 and BB814, (The 'invisible' members of the flight).

Every year in November the Royal Navy have a ceremony to commemorate the Taranto operation and in 1962 LS326 was hoisted aboard *H.M.S. Hermes* to act as the centrepiece to the celebrations. Apparently, in the way of these events, the alcohol was flowing freely, and it subsequently transpired that Lt. Cdr. 'Lofty' Wrenford, the pilot of LS326 had been buttonholed by guest of honour Lord Louis Mountbatten who had suggested that rather than ignominiously being winched off the carrier, it would be more fitting if the aircraft was flown off two days later when *Hermes* would be at sea. Luckily for posterity, Brian Johnson of the B.B.C. was invited aboard the Swordfish for this one-off flight on November 13th as he recounts:

Stringbaggers

WARBIRDS WORLDWIDE
TWENTY NINE

Battle Honours

The Bismarck Raid, The Channel Dash Fiasco & Eugene Esmonde

When the German battleship Bismarck was on the high seas, it was imperative that it was brought to battle by a British fleet, and destroyed. After a positively cinematic chase, the Bismarck was attacked by a flight of Swordfish from HMS Victorious, led by Lt. Cdr. Eugene Esmonde RN (after they had earlier attacked HMS Sheffield in error, and the Captain of Sheffield pointed out that their torpedoes were exploding prematurely).In later strikes by Swordfish from HMS Ark Royal, several torpedo hits were scored by these fifteen valiant crews of 810, 818 and 820 Squadrons against a huge amount of flak and in filthy weather, one torpedo jamming the Bismarck's rudder, stopping the great ship's evasions and enabling the Royal Navy's 'Force H' to attack and finally sink her. Another veteran Stringbag pilot said "Try to imagine the scene - these nine paper-and-string joke-planes flying unescorted, in daylight, to strike the world's most powerful warship,"

This incredible achievement coming after the miraculous Taranto attack, may have led the Admiralty to believe that the Swordfish and its crews were in some way invincible. When the Scharnhorst and Gneisenau ran up the Channel to escape to Norway, in one of the most bungled operations of the war, six Swordfish of 825 Sqn, commanded by Lt. Cdr. Eugene Esmonde were sent to attack these ships. Because of mistiming, the RAF escort was not able to cover the 825 Sqn attack, All six aircraft were shot down by flak and Luftwaffe fighters, only five of the eighteen crew surviving. Eugene Esmonde was awarded a posthumous Victoria Cross(the Fleet Air Arm's first in World War II) for an operation which should never have been attempted; and the Swordfish was never used as a torpedo bomber again.

Taranto

In the thirties. when the future of Naval power was still under some doubt, and the idea of 'a Fleet in Being' dominated naval strategy, even the possibility of naval aircraft being a decisive factor was out of all possibility. When it became evident that the modern Italian fleet were not prepared to enter a decisive battle with the outnumbered Royal Navy in the Mediterranean, a plan conceived by Admiral Sir Lumley Lister in the late 'thirties was brought off the shelf and dusted down. The intention was to attack the Italians from the air alone in their main naval base (Taranto harbour) and endeavour to sink as many of their capital ships as possible. To do this, there was the brand new carrier HMS Illustrious; the antique carrier HMS Eagle (which went unserviceable before the raid, but loaned a Squadron of aircraft to Illustrious) 21 Fairey Swordfish torpedo bombers and the 18 inch torpedo with a new, untried 'duplex' fuse. It was a recipe for disaster.

On the night of November 11/12, 1940, two strikes of twelve and nine Swordfish went in against a massive amount of anti-aircraft fire to drop their torpedoes and bombs in the crowded confines of Taranto harbour. Up to a hundred percent casualties were expected as this type of operation was totally new. Incredibly, of the twenty-one aircraft sent only one was lost with both crewmen, while another crew were picked up by the Italians after their aircraft was shot down. The Italians had three battleships sunk, damage to two cruisers and further damage was caused to two fleet auxiliaries, the seaplane base and oil storage depot.

The full story of the Taranto attack is an epic of Naval warfare;success had been achieved by the incredible skill, training and expertise of all the Naval personnel involved. The cream of the pre-war Fleet Air Arm, many would be killed within the next few months, yet a decisive battle had wrest the initiative from the Italians. Significantly, aboard the carrier Illustrious was a United States Navy observer, Lt. Cdr. Opie, while in Japan, the Japanese naval staff quietly collated the details, planned and looked closely at the Pacific Naval base of Pearl Harbour.

In one half-hour attack, the future of naval aviation was assured; the balance of power in the Mediterranean Theatre changed irrevocably, and the Fleet Air Arm gained a battle honour as great as that of Trafalgar. Admiral Cunningham stated that the Swordfish had "inflicted more damage upon the Italian fleet than was inflicted on the German high seas fleet at the battle of Jutland."

The Stringbaggers

"In 1962, surviving World War two aircraft were not, perhaps, considered the priceless jewels they are today; further, the term "airworthy", as then applied to preserved military aircraft, had, shall we say, a certain elasticity of interpretation. It was certainly one thing to potter *en fete* round an airfield circuit and quite another to take off from a carrier out of sight of land, when being supported and sustained solely by the biplane's one and only Pegasus engine that had several of its major components "acquired" from various static, not to say scrap examples."

At 1400 hrs, on November 13th, 1962, the wheels of LS326 rolled on what was the last ever takeoff from a carrier by a Swordfish. After a rather protracted return to Lee on Solent:

"Naval 326, Field in sight..." The minutes ticked by.........

'Lee to Naval 326, Are you a helicopter?'
'Negative,' replied Lofty coldly, 'A Swordfish.'"

Another small piece of history made, In the nature of the Senior Service, creating traditions was something that just 'happened', Part of LS326's display routine nowadays is a slow flyby with the crew (pilot excepted) standing at attention and saluting the crowd, while the white ensign flies from the cockpit. Not so well know is that this tradition dates back to May 28th 1964, when on the occasion of the Fleet Air Arm review at Yeovilton the crew decided to salute the reviewer, on this occasion HRH Prince Philip, as similarly presented ground forces would do. Of course, on such an auspicious occasion, all the senior personnel were wheeled out, and it was with no lesser a pilot aboard than Rear Admiral P.D. Gick that the Swordfish was to set this precedent, All three crew members had flown together twenty-five years previously, and with Rear-Admiral H.R.V. Janvrin and Lt. Cdr. C. Topliss aboard the combined age of the crew totalled over 150 years. As this salute went down so well it became part of the show routine with this origin of the event later lost in the mists of time!

Less obvious in origin is a rather strange piece of apparel that can be donned by one of LS326's 'lookers'. While the open cockpit of the Stringbag makes exceptional demands on the dress standards of its crew, the requirement for an aviation type solar topee with the cut down brim may not,at first glance,seem all that odd, Nevertheless, the addition of a flashing red beacon on the top is somewhat unique as a way of alerting other traffic as to the presence of a unique aircraft; but it works by golly, it works.

The Fleet Air Arm Museum meanwhile had acquired their own static Swordfish (HS618, previously painted as 'W5984' now as 'P4139') from Donibristle, and thus LS326 was no longer threatened with being mummified in a museum, Nevertheless, efforts to keep LS326 airworthy were becoming increasingly frustrated by problems with the Pegasus engine which was simply becoming worn out. After years for searching the world for replacement Pegasus engines, (a similar search is currently being carried out by Dick Melton for his Supermarine Walrus restoration) an answer was found at Lambeth, South London. In 1965 a deal was concluded with the Imperial War Museum to acquire the Pegasus on their aircraft, NF370 and the spare the I.W.M. held in store, the RNHF providing the I.W.M. with a static, but complete engine for their aircraft. As was to be expected this windfall did not make an instantly airworthy engine, but with over 550 man-hours and considerable help from Rolls-Royce Bristol, including the manufacture of parts and tools, a 'new' engine, good for 500 hours, was available to be hung on the front end of Stringbag LS326. This was none too soon, as '326 had suffered a partial engine failure' after leaving Booker Aerodrome from a display, and the aircraft was grounded until the end of the year, The new engine was cranked into life on January 17th 1970, and

Continued on Page 30

Below: Swordfish NF389 in its airworthy days with the Fleet Air Arm (APN via James Kightly)

My involvement with HS469 began a couple of years ago when an engineer from the Canadian Armed Forces base at Shearwater, Nova Scotia, visited the RN Historic flight at Yeovilton. He was looking for information and some parts and tools to help with the reconstruction of Swordfish HS469. We managed to organise visits to British Aerospace at Brough to see W5856 during reconstruction, and Rolls-Royce at Filton who were rebuilding two Pegasus engines for us. Additionally we were able to help with a few bits and bobs, copied manuals, talked, drank beer and let him have a good look over the engineless LS326. At that stage he asked if I would fly their Swordfish project when it was finished and I naturally jumped at the chance. I was subsequently formally invited by first the Curator of the Shearwater museum and then the Director, a serving Canadian Forces Colonel who also Commands a Helicopter Squadron (shades of Historic Flight there!).

The project started life as a very poorly hulk in a farm at Lynville, Ontario. Trees had grown up through the fuselage, the undercarriage had sunk into the ground, and many parts were missing. To add a little wartime colour, local riflemen had used it for target practice! The original, aptly nicknamed 'the Stringbaggers', were given permission in 1980 to purchase that hulk and another they had located, and begin work under the auspices of the Shearwater Museum. Work commenced, painfully slowly in a totally unheated waterfront building in Torc harbour, (served by a single 13 amp electric outlet). Early in the project the team decided that if the aircraft was to mean anything at all it would have to fly. They set to with that in mind and with Brian Aston as Chief Engineer,(who was employed as a Department of Transport accident investigator), each stage was carefully brought up to airworthy standard and certified. Brian's background and obvious desire not to become one of his own customers has meant a lot to me in the build up to the first flight!

Moves were made from the original shed to first a small and then larger and more apt space at CFB Downsview(Toronto), where work progressed well. Large assemblies had to be fabricated from new tubing, sheet or plate, using the original unsound parts or drawings as patterns. Many parts that could not be fabricated had to be located and purchased or traded. In August 1990 HS469 once again looked like an aeroplane and was formally rolled out at Downsview.Despite one or two borrowed parts it looked fabulous and had all of the requisite paperwork to fly. However, the engine was another matter, still requiring some assembly work and missing a Townend ring (exhaust to the uninitiated). Shortly after roll out the entire project was flown by C-130 to Shearwater in time to be a static exhibit at the International Air Show in September. Whilst this was good progress for the museum, the aircraft was now 1200 miles away from the retired Canadian Fleet Air Arm personnel who

Top: Shearwater Swordfish HS469 groundrunning. Below: The exhilarating moment of lift off, first time since 1946! (both via John Beattie)

John Beattie reports on Test flying HS469, the second Canadian Swordfish rebuild

Shearwater
Swordfish
Canada's latest airworthy Stringbag

Shearwater Swordfish

had spent so many hours bringing her this far, and Brian was spending a lot of his time at his home in England's Lake District!

A brand new Townend ring was manufactured by IMP at Halifax airport from stainless steel and is a tribute to their ingenuity and craftsmanship, though very expensive. Brake bags were manufactured and certified locally by a tiny company, something we have been trying to achieve in England for years now. A good many other 'insurmountable' problems were overcome by good engineering practice, rugged determination, native cunning and all those other attributes essential to the re-creators of old flying machines.

Things looked good for a flying date in August 1993 to be set, and this coincided with the rededication of an old building as the new Shearwater Museum. The team assembled and I was summoned from summer leave in Somerset, but alas the technical problems piled up and although they were whittled away one by one, they proved too great. The aircraft *looked* tremendous and was very close to being serviceable. The team had put in two weeks of early mornings and late nights but we all ran out of time and had to disappear to Toronto, the Lake District and in my case Elvington Air Show in W5856! We did make a tentative date to do it all again in the spring.

I was about to leave the Navy and on terminal leave visiting my daughter in New Zealand when the call came, ... a bit like the Gumball' film I suppose,...."it's on, we need you 4th April to 15th April". Re negotiation got them 7th to 14th, but still meant I had to miss the Wanaka airshow! The aircraft had run fairly successfully a couple of times but was not yet performing quite to specification. I got home on 5th April and in the evening a quiet Canadian voice on my telephone asked if it was possible to bring a Carburettor with me? Historic flight had just got our two Swordfish running properly for the season and were not amused. There was no spare carb. However, they did understand the problem and had been grateful many times for help we had received from many quarters and so agreed that I could borrow LS326s, but don't bother coming home if it gets broken and/or fails to work when refitted! The Canadians promised faithfully not to touch any settings and I eased the enormous chunk of a Claudel Hobson twin upchoke Carb into my grip to carry as hand baggage. The security at Heathrow were very good, though did X Ray it four or five times,......I'm not sure whether out of interest or looking for cracks!

On arrival in Canada I discovered they had found a number of induction leaks and were about to run it again with their Carb fitted in the hope that they had cured the faults. Utilising a battery powered electric drill to turn the booster generator (to provide a fat spark at very low RPM) and a Harvard starter motor, it started very easily, but they hadn't

fixed it......it popped and banged, failed to accelerate evenly and one magneto was dead. Off came the mag and went to the local mag man who was more used to those from Continentals, but he did fix the fault. Carbs were exchanged and the next run was very much better, though there was a noticeable vibration from the prop in the mid speed range. This was fixed by machining up a new cone washer and torquing down the prop bolts. Now the business of clocking up enough hours to fulfil the Rolls Royce established ground test programme. After an hour of perfect running it made quite a bang and spat out lots of oil; calamity when things appeared to be on the turn. Oil level wasn't down much and it turned freely with no naughty clanks (that in itself is unusual!), so we ran it again. Brian noticed the fault almost as soon as it started,.......the crankcase breather pipe, manufactured out of 1 inch steel braided flexy hose, was pointing into the prop wash and obviously pressurising the crankcase. I had similar bangs when 326's engine had lost a cylinder in 1991. It all made sense, so we repositioned the breather and the next couple of runs were faultless. During the ground running I had discovered a couple of things about the cockpit which could have been better and certainly weren't original, (a) the Airspeed indicator was 0 to 250 knots, but the section I was interested in, from 0 to 100 knots occupied less than 1/4 of the scale and (b) the RPM gauge was 1200 to 3500 RPM, when I was interested in 400 to 2300, though at least it did cover 1/2 the scale. The landing lamp knob also obscured that vital 1/4 of the ASI face, but I soon cured that myself by taking it off.

So, we were now ready for the off and last minute preps were made, which included George Cummins busily stripping and reassembling the complicated brake valve several times to no avail. Air leaked out of the accumulator and the compressor wouldn't top it up, ...time again for native cunning even though I did assure them that brakes were really not necessary. A Sub Aqua bottle and regulator was introduced to the system, just in case'. It worked OK in the hangar but never did once out of the door! The flying controls had been a little stiff and large quantities of oil were poured into every bit that moved and I sat during my ground running time exercising them liberally. It seemed to work.

The rest of the team turned up from Toronto on the night of 12th April and immediately donned overalls and those of us not gainfully employed in the more technical matters washed her down of the months of collected dust, oil and other unsightly contaminants. A few beers later on that night helped to allay any further fears that she might not fly. The morning of 13th was set for the final 'proof' ground run, required before she could fly. Various powers are set and readings taken, up to full power. On the Swordfish the Boost control allows up to +1/2 psi in 'Altitude' setting and +2 psi in 'Rich'. Both were achieved without resetting, and she sailed through the 'slam' checks during which, whilst wincing, you open the throttle from idle to full power in three seconds. It never seems fair to an old engine to treat it that roughly and in service I'm sure we don't, but I suppose you have to prove that you can apply power quickly to get out of trouble without the engine 'rich-cutting'. With the ground run out of the way I went across to 406 Squadron to be given an 'airfield famil' in a Sea King. As an ex Sea King pilot I was very pleased at this and had an excellent time. Air traffic next for a briefing with the controller and the Operations Officer, where we discussed the wind, runways, other

traffic, radio procedures with my hand held ground only set and so on. The germ of an idea was laid to do a flyby with an F-18 who was visiting, which didn't come off for some reason, and I floated the idea of a mixed formation with Sea King and T-33, but that fell on stony ground too - oh well.

So, take off time came round quickly and we towed HS469 out to the threshold of the runway (with no brakes, you can't taxi). She started beautifully and we warmed her up slowly. Brian Aston was to travel with me as flight test engineer, our authority only allowing 'essential crew'. He took some readings from the back but it was quite difficult as there was no intercom, and during the flight I wrote some down and remembered others. I do have to say at this stage the full test flight would not be possible as a number of the systems were not in commission,...no compressor, generator, suction pump and the slats were locked in (they having been assessed as too stiff in operation). Staring eagerly down the 9000ft of runway we did the final run up at 1800 RPM and mag drop, just within limits on the weak mag, but quite even and good steady oil pressure, no popping or banging and smooth deceleration to an even tick over.

Wind was about 15kts, with a little crosswind from the right. Also on the right runway edge a small fleet of vehicles with cameramen and Colonel Cody, the Station Commander. Not a good time to screw up! Chocks away and she didn't move at tick over,...good, that probably means she will stop when we get back without having to shut down the engine. Smooth application of throttle to about half power in 'Rich setting, keep straight with rudder, no problem so ease the power in to about 0 Boost and lift the tail to the flying attitude, check that she is making about 2100 RPM, she is. Controls feel good, but only 8500 ft of con-

crete left so ease back on the stick at about 65 kts and she flies! Didn't need all of that runway after all. Beautiful....... controls work as they should, trim feels nice, engine working faultlessly, all T's and P's in the green and I have even avoided hitting the Station Commander - wonderful. Slight moment of hesitation when the realisation dawns that you won't get back onto the runway if the motor quits, and everyone knows about turnbacks from low level. Every direction is full of trees except the Lake to the North, be brave, the moment passes and we're up to 1000ft over the far end of the runway, moving the mixture into Altitude', and turning to the downwind. The sortie had been planned to be conducted in the overhead in a wide orbit such that an engine out landing to the field could be made if necessary, *and* we wore parachutes - well you never know-

THE TEST ITSELF

First exercise the throttle to ensure response is normal, letting the engine settle down at cruise power and carry out a few turns to establish whether there are any unusual handling tendencies. All is well, so into the height climb, which measures the achieved rate of climb between one and four thousand feet at full power in the altitude setting. She makes about 1000ft per minute (which reassuringly is the same as ours) and the engine T's and P's remain steady and well within limits. At the top of the climb move the mixture back into Rich and let her settle for a minute or two at -2 Boost- All normal, so ease up to full power and leave it there for a minute or so. She makes +2 Boost with rock steady oil pressure and temperature well below the line. Back to 0 Boost and see how fast she'll go - around 115 kts. Then fly at 90 kts and see how much power she uses, about -2 Boost. At all of these settings note readings from the engine instruments- Now gaining a little confidence in the engine and begin the handling element. Dive to max speed (artificially set at 130 kts, in service it was 206, but must have required quite a steep dive to achieve it). Check for flutter and aileron up float (not expected at 130 I must say) and generally move the stick around to assess feel and rates of roll and pitch. She does feel very good indeed. Next the stall, if you can get it to! Pull back the power to idle for the first time since take off, note with relief that the engine still runs and bring the speed back, trimming to the aft stop in the process, but having reached the aft stop putting a couple of generous handfuls of forward trim back in. The 'stall' in the Swordfish is difficult to determine, but I reckon it was around 54kts. Trying to do the same from higher speed but in the turn gets the same result as with ours, the speed washes off as you pull into the turn, but just when you KNOW it will stall the nose drops a degree or two and it picks up a couple of knots! A sort of low speed yo yo. Anyway,

the check is about ensuring that she won't flick into or out of the turn or into a spin. Perfect in both directions. Wind down the "flaps", which on the 'Fish is a large hand wheel at the rear of the centre upper wing has the effect of drooping the ailerons eight degrees. It may have made a difference flying to a MAC ship, but it has - effect of making the aircraft stiff and awkward in roll. Wind those back up again. A couple of mild wingovers completes test and it is time to formate with a Canadian Sea King to have our picture taken before descending back into the circuit. Funnily enough the performance of the Sea King is remarkably similar to the 'Fish. Anti submarine role and with a radar fit similar weapon loads, level speed, load carrying capacity, so on. The 'Fish couldn't hover and I don't think the Sea King could dive bomb at 206, plus a generation or two of technology gap of course, but the basic parameters are not unalike.

ATC have cleared a T-33 to land and I watch him round out on runway 16 and note that the wind has increased slightly and is almost 90 degrees crosswind on that runway. This is not good without brakes; as the aircraft slows down it weather cocks into wind. I ask for runway 25 and get approval. 25 gives a slight crosswind from the left which is fine and the approach is over the lake, which seems very fitting and appropriate for a Swordfish to be flying over, (though at the last minute I realise that although we have parachutes we don't have lifejackets,....be brave!). 25 is considerably shorter than 16, but as we reckon to put a 'Fish down and stop in less than 2500ft without brakes, at 6000ft it is plenty. The approach is commenced at about 80 kts and despite the engine being in the way, the view is always quite good, looking through the top two cylinders on late finals. Being a large and 'draggy' aircraft she handles docilely on the approach and is quite speed stable if kept in trim. Throttle is used to set or adjust rate of descent, 1100 to 1300 RPM being normal, giving around 300 Feet per minute. The speed is washed back to 70 kts, slightly higher than normal because of the locked slats, and the engine brought gently back to idle at about ten feet. Landing is a doddle, just try and keep her level at five to ten feet and she gently sinks to the tarmac as speed and thus lift reduces, with no bounce at all. During the roll out a gentle turn to the left develops despite full right rudder, but that is turned into a gentle turn to the right with full right rudder and just the tinniest bit of power. By the time the turn is left again we are almost stopped and another squeeze of power is all that is needed prior to stopping inside 2000ft from touchdown. The ground crew arrive and chock the aircraft and the throttle is eased up to 1100 RPM for one minutes gentle cooling before shutdown.

After a very careful counting of the pieces

Shearwater Swordfish

and assuring that nothing had worked loose or appeared to be in any way stressed, we readied for the official press call that evening. Weather the next day was going to be awful, and this was not an awful weather aeroplane any more! Additionally I had to head back to the U.K. to learn to be a civilian and needed to take RNHF carb with me. Cameras rolled, shutters clicked, breath was held. Calamity during the start, the booster coil electric drill came off and could not be put back on without removing the top engine cover, an aluminium work of art the size of a small marquee. Without the electric drill she would not start. Added to this crisis, the Harvard electric starter that replaced the two sailors as the means of turning the engine, had started making terminal death dive noises. The only thing to do was start the engine without the top cover, and put it on later! This was achieved, just as the aforementioned Harvard part gave up the ghost, on the second attempt. Warm up was normal and then came the moment for four lumberjacks to put on the top cover. This they achieved but in the process rendered two more of the fasteners inoperative (become knackered). Once again ingenuity and native cunning came to the fore and a large roll of strong masking tape was wound round the complete nose section to ensure security. Happy with the outcome, I had a very enjoyable 15 minutes running through a low level display or two, which I have to say was aimed more at the 'Stringbaggers' and Canadian Navy than the press! Now confident that all was well with her, I flew a crisp display using up to about 80 degrees of bank and around 25 degrees nose up and down. It did feel good and I considered myself very lucky to be there. Thank you Canadian Authorities for insisting someone with 'recent Swordfish experience' be the first to fly her.

HS469 came alive once again and whilst some of her systems were not functioning, the vital ones were, and she passed her first test flight in 48 years with flying colours and to the original specification. She was a delight to fly and I got an enormous feeling of pride at being associated with the project. The team who had rebuilt her were tremendous to be with, full of that indomitable spirit and humour, associated with naval aviation. The back up they received from all departments at Shearwater, certainly in the time I was there, was impressive by any standards. The Stringbaggers have made a significant personal achievement and given the world another of those fantastic old aeroplanes that had enjoyed such a distinguished operational career in days when results really mattered. 469 will now go into the museum at Shearwater as their star exhibit but with no plans to fly again..........yet!
WW John Beattie.

Stringbaggers
Continued from Page 26

LS326 was able to return to the skies once again. Not only did it have a new Peggy aboard, but from the parts left over from their years of scrounging and making do, as well as the injection of new items from the I.W.M. and Rolls-Royce the Flight set about assembling a spare engine.

And so the unique aircraft continued to build up the hours, appearing at air displays all over the United Kingdom. Flying a single-engined open-cockpit biplane antiquated even in the warbird world does make some additional demands upon the crew, not least the ability to stand up to freezing, howling gales in the rear cockpit as well as an ability to get up earlier than everyone so as to arrive at the correct slot time.

In 1987, it was apparent that everyday wear and tear over the considerable number of years meant that a large amount of work was necessary to refresh LS326's tired airframe and engineer, CPO Alastair MacKay initiated an engineering programme of stripping down LS326 for a complete overhaul. As the aircraft had parts removed and inspected, it quickly became apparent that it was not just a question of paint-stripping the panels, bashing out some dents and recovering the airframe; a good deal more replacement and remanufacture was to be necessary, Luckily, *Personal Plane Services* at Booker were prepared to undertake some of the work necessary and to provide hangarage while this went on, meanwhile the

Above: Two RNHF Swordfish together for the first time at BAe Brough (David Stephens)

normal RNHF crew got on with the many other tasks the refurbishment required, Again new flying and lifting wires were sought. Bruntons of Musselbrough supplying the rare items to order on this occasion.

It had been discovered sometime earlier that Swordfish LS326 had been being coy about her wartime service, and far from the unglamorous role of being used as a training hack, it transpired she had served aboard the MAC Ship Escort Carrier *S.S. Rapana* with 836 Sqn, 'L' Flight on a convoy to Nova Scotia in company with two sister Swordfish in October 1943. On her return to the UK LS326 was damaged in a flying accident and thus her less combative (but already documented) role with Station flights was to commence.

As a result of this new information, it was naturally decided to return LS326 to her own authentic colours, those she had been wearing until 1987 being a mixture made up of a 1940 scheme corrupted to a 1942 variant, bearing '5A' on the rudder and having acquired a set of invasion stripes for the 40th anniversary of D-Day (when she had been one of the aircraft to overfly Arromanche beach on the 6th of June)all of which was less than correct for any Swordfish, This was just one of the limitations

Above: The scene at British Aerospace Brough where Swordfish W5856 nestles in with a classic modern day naval fighter. British Aerospace are keen supporters of the RNHF (BAe Brough photograph).

set by the fact that the Historic Flight receives no government support.

Thanks to the research carried out by Mike Keep and Ian Huntley, the scheme was worked

out in detail and paint was supplied by Messrs Trimite Ltd., mixed to the correct wartime hue specifications, though in semi-matt cellulose to match the wartime type 'S' (for Smooth) that most MAC ship Swordfish wore.

The strain of being the only airworthy Stringbag was obviously proving too much for the old girl, as on 14th of June 1991, the faithful Pegasus engine threw a cylinder while pilot Lt. Cdr. Beattie was undertaking a test flight over Somerset at 2500 feet. He was successful in force landing the aircraft at Henstridge, and the engine was rebuilt by Rolls-Royce at Filton. The engine was back on LS326 in July 92, undertaking test runs and the aircraft took to the air once more in August of that year. Swordfish LS326 was not to be alone for much longer though, as Bob Spence had flown his Swordfish C-GEVS HS554 in Canada, and though temporarily robbed of its own engine to assist with the restoration of LS326's the airframe of W5856 at British Aerospace Brough was making good progress to airworthy condition for the flight.

Fairey Swordfish Mk II W5856 (G-BMGC)
Back in seventies the Strathallan Collection of Sir William Roberts was forging ahead with an innovative and imaginative collecting policy and they had the not unreasonable aim of restoring types as varied as the Westland

Let's Get 'em Flying!

The Stringbaggers

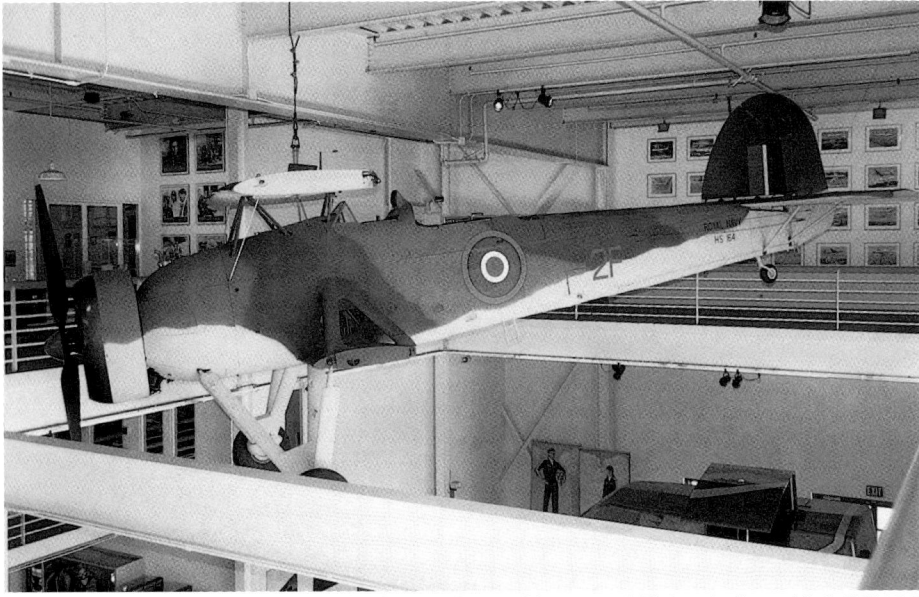

Above: Hanging from the roof at the Santa Monica Museum of Flying is Swordfish 'HS164' (Mark Ansell). Below: Swordfish NF839 in all her glory on static display at Yeovilton (Mark Ansell).

Lysander, Bristol Bolingbroke, Fairey Battle and Fairey Swordfish to the air. Sadly, only the Lysander was totally restored, and the Swordfish airframe that Strathallan had brought from Canada, was sold to the *Swordfish Heritage Trust* in 1990, after a certain amount of work had been done on the machine.

The airframe was received at British Aerospace Brough, Humberside (which had been a Blackburn factory) on December 14th 1990, As another of the 1699 'Blackfish' built, W5856 was rebuilt by BAe wearing their 'Blackburn's hat'. A team of restorers was formed from BAe employees, headed by Graham Chisnall, and three staff were allocated full time to the project. The 750 hp Bristol Pegasus engine went to Rolls-Royce Flight Systems at Filton, Bristol for rebuilding, coming back to Brough as a nearly new unit. Initial inspection revealed that the windscreen and frame, braking system and exhaust ring, as well as a number of instruments were missing, not a bad minimum,

Work was set to at a cracking pace at Brough, kicking off with the testing and X-raying being carried out, something that Brough were ideally placed to undertake, and an aspect that had caused Strathallan to behave with caution as there was some doubt as to the integrity of the mainspars, due to evidence of minor corrosion. Despite this deterioration of the airframe, quickly repaired, no major components such as the spars or longerons needed major work, and this enabled the restoration to speed ahead, the entire project being completed within an incredible three year time span. Lack of paper information led the Brough workers to inspect the I.W.M. Swordfish at Duxford and then the Lee-On-Solent aircraft NF389 was transported to Brough to enable comparative examinations of parts and configurations to be carried out. The I.W.M. machine donated its windscreen to enable a new example to be fabricated for W5856. The decision was taken to make the instrument panel on W5856 match that of LS326 as nearly as possible, to enable pilot currency between the two aircraft to be easily maintained, This led to the rather unusual situation where non-Swordfish (but still antiquated) instruments had to be found and fitted; and while those aboard LS326 were probably current Royal Navy equipment when scrounged by the RNHF - in the l990's they make an odd selection themselves; comprising a RPM indicator from a deHavilland Dove (or Devon) Engine Temperature System from a Hawker Seahawk, and the Oil Pressure Indicator from a deHavilland Chipmunk. Each of these veteran units had to then be re configured to be fitted to the 'new' Swordfish.

As the RNHF was intending to have both Swordfish on strength simultaneously, the decision was taken for W5856 to have a paint scheme as different from that of LS326 as possible, The pre-war colours of an aircraft aboard H.M.S. Ark Royal were chosen, and the overall silver scheme, relieved by the blue-red-blue sash of Royal Marine Captain Nigel Skene, CO of 810 TSR(Torpedo Spotter Reconnaissance) Squadron was that selected. The unmistakable ensemble is completed by the black and white

Below: The spartan cockpit of Swordfish LS326 - note the spade grip control column. It makes the achievements of the aircraft and crew over the years all the more remarkable.

Left: Both RNHF Swordfish - LS326 and W5856 at Duxford's D-Day show on 3rd May 94 (James Kightly).

striped fin and rudder and 1939 summer air exercise identifying yellow stripe down the fuselage side. This vibrantly colourful coat is added to by the logo of British Aerospace on the fin, As BAe had made a major contribution to the survival and airworthiness of W5856, they would like to have it referred to as the 'BAe Swordfish' and to confuse matters further, being a Blackburn machine, it would be perfectly correct (though rather obscure) to refer to W5856 as the BAe Blackfish!

The first flight of W5856 took place on May 12th 1993 in the hands of Lt. Cdr. John Beattie, then CO of the RNHF. It lasted 45 minutes, and along with a few successive flights it was possible to fill all the paperwork requirements and give flights to the restoration team.

First flying on October 21st 1941, W5856 had served during the war, with various units in the European theatre before being shipped to Canada. Starting with anti-shipping duties while based at Malta, experimental and training work was followed by anti-'E' and 'R' Boat operations over the Channel in 1944 - all cut short by a forced landing in February 1944, after which, repaired, the machine was crated and shipped to Canada. Its Canadian service occurred at Yarmouth, Nova Scotia.

On May 22nd 1993, Fairey Swordfish Mk II W5856 was handed over to Rear Admiral Ian Garnett, Flag Officer Naval Aviation, representing the Royal Navy Historic Flight, by Mr. Dick Evans, Chief Executive of British Aerospace. The opportunity was then taken to put two Swordfish into the air simultaneously for the first time probably since the *Sink the Bismarck* filming, LS326 being flown by Lt Cdr David Knight and W5856 in the hands of Captain Simon Thornewill DSC.

The Other Survivors

While Swordfish Mk.II LS326 had been flying the flag in Britain (for many years alone) it was not the only survivor by any mean, As mentioned earlier, the Imperial War Museum had an example, NF370, which was getting increasingly badly vandalised in a carrier hanger-lift diorama at their main base at Lambeth. In the early 'Nineties the now very patched airframe was transferred to Duxford while Lambeth itself underwent refurbishment and though a major strip down of the airframe was undertaken to establish what state the airframe was in was started, work on her appears to have halted, though BAe had a good look at her while restoring W5856. No doubt in due course the machine will take a place in the extensive rebuild programme of the I.W.M.

The R.A.F., Muscum acquired a derelict ex-Canadian example of a Fairey Swordfish Mk.IV, for many years believed to be anonymous. even receiving the *British Aircraft Preservation Council* (B.A.P.C.) number 108 as a result of its mysterious origins. In depth digging has since revealed the serial of HS503 which is believed correct: and this airframe resides with the RAF Museum reserve collection at Cosford after moving from Henlow.

In the U.S.A., there is one wingless example at the *Santa Monica Museum of Flying*, displayed suspended from the ceiling as 'HS164', another ex-Ernie Simmons airframe; and effectively a semi-anonymous one.

The extensive and effective collecting policy of the *Canadian War Museum* enabled them to acquire a Swordfish in 1965 from Ernie Simmons before his death, and this aircraft, as no serial could be found, one was selected at random. It was restored to static condition by the *Fairey Aviation Company of Canada Ltd.*, with assistance from the Royal Canadian Navy, as NS122 'TH-M', in which colours it is currently displayed as part of the *Canadian National Aeronautical Collection* at Rockcliffe.

Tough, dependable, rugged, vital and so often the right aircraft at the right time, the Swordfish inspired an affection in its crews that few other types could. There can be no better recommendation for an aircraft. Next time you see one of the world's four airworthy machines fly by, or stop by and look up at a static survivor, give a thought to those crews who made history at Taranto, tackled the latest German battleship, or flew any of the millions of sorties performed in sub-zero temperatures for hour after hour protecting convoys, patrolling the seas and hunting submarines. The Senior Service once had 'wooden ships and iron men'; there is no doubt that the Swordfish follows in that arduous tradition.
WW James Kightly

To book the Fairey Swordfish of the Royal Naval Historic Flight, contact Barbara Broadwater at RNAS Yeovilton, Ilchester, Somerset BA22 8HT, Tel (0935) 456725. Fax (0935) 455273.

Acknowledgments

We would like to thank a number of people who have helped to make this feature as extensive as it is. They are as follows - Mike Baker; John Beattie (R.N. Ret'd); Barbara Broadwater of the Royal Navy Historic Flight; Graham Duck of BAe Brough; Lt Cdr Hugh Deuxberry and Lt Cdr David Lord RNHF, CO Heron Flight: Ian Huntley: John Laurijssen of the Swordfish Heritage Trust; Norman Pealing; Dianne Seager, University of Waterloo, and David Stephens.

SWORDFISH VIDEO

For those interested in the Stringbag a video is available from the RNHF. It shows every fascinating aspect of the rebuild of W5856 - engine and airframe. Review in WW30! 60 minutes Colour/Black & White Price £12.00 + £2.00 p&p from:
RN Historic Flight, RNAS Yeovilton, Ilchester, Somerset BA22 8HT

Below: The handover of Swordfish W5856's logbooks at British Aerospace Brough

Fishbed 21

Top: Sonic Aviation's MiG-21UM accompanied by an FA-18 Hornet of 77Sqn. near Williamtown RAAF Base during the MiG's first flight on 2nd March 1994 (RAAF Official Cpl Andy Hall). *Left:* Squadron Leader Phil Frawley, designated pilot for the MiG's first flight (Peter Anderson). *Above:* MiG-21 over the sea near Williamtown (RAAF Official Cpl Andy Hall).

Peter N. Anderson reports on Australia's entry into supersonic jet operations with the first flight of **Sonic Aviation's** MiG-21UM, rebuilt by **Winrye Aviation**

At 1051hrs on 2nd March 1994, the Australian warbird movement entered the supersonic era with the first post restoration flight of the *Sonic Aviation Syndicate's* MiG-21UM.

The aircraft, S/N 51-6905011, was imported during September 1992 by Ansett Airlines 767 Captain Dick Macintosh direct from Poland where it had served its operational life attached to a reconnaissance squadron. During the twenty odd years since its manufacture in 1969 the MiG had accumulated only 1422 hrs total time giving an average utilisation of barely 60 hours per annum and, as a result, the airframe is in excellent condition.

Notwithstanding its general appearance and low hours, the machine was moved to *Winrye Aviation* at Bankstown Airport for a complete systems overhaul together with the modifications necessary for civilian operation.

Although it had been manufactured as a UM model, the aircraft is fitted with the two pylon wing and R11Fs-300 engine more common to the U and US series of MiG-21 trainers. However, all other systems reflect the UM model including the instructors' rear cockpit periscope, angle of attack sensor, upgraded avionics, instrumentation and the KM-1 ejection seats. As a result of these factory fitted variations it was necessary not only to undertake the aircraft's civil certification but also to carry out a complete systems analysis to ascertain any other minor departures from the standard UM to satisfy CAA requirements.

Due to the aircraft's performance characteristics, it had been decided from the outset that the rocket ejection seats were to be 'live'. Having regard to the recently introduced U.S. F.A.A. requirements regarding the arming of ejection seats, many anticipated that the proposed live seats would prove a major stumbling block for the restoration. Nevertheless, protracted negotiations with the Civil Aviation Authority finally resulted in CAA agreement to the use of both the live seats and parachute

Above: The MiG-21 lifts off for its first flight under the command of Squadron Leader Phil Frawley RAAF. Below: The aircraft on a low loader prior to unloading at Sydney's Kingsford Smith airport (P.Anderson).

braking system thereby paving the way for the activation of these emergency lifesaving devices on other Australian high performance civilian aircraft.

During the rebuild, the MiG provided its fair share of challenges for *Winrye*, not the least of which was the installation of civilian avionics in an airframe having virtually no unoccupied space. This installation proved time consuming but was eventually achieved with a minimum of modification and by employing part of the MiGs existing avionics suite.

In addition to the avionics and systems upgrades carried out by *Winrye* and despite its

AUSTRALIAN MiG-21

Fishbed 21

Right: The front cockpit showing active gunsight and detailed work carried out by Winrye. despite the generally good condition of the aircraft upon arrival at Winrye both cockpits were completely stripped out, repainted in a stock peacock blue and refitted with control panel detailing and placards in English. (Peter Anderson).

generally excellent condition, the cockpit area unquestionably reflected the aircraft's previous military life. As a result, both cockpits were completely stripped and repainted in their original peacock blue scheme and all switches and control panels were detailed and re-placarded in English. To further enhance the originality of the cockpit area, the ASP gunsight was also retained, detailed and returned to fully operational condition.

After considerable deliberation, the paint scheme finally chosen for the aircraft was based on the Indian Air Force *Red Archers* aerobatic team markings of the early 1970s. Little information and no colour photographs were available for the preparation of this striking scheme and it was necessary to contact former team members in India in order to fully research the final colour and markings details. Although the *Red Archers* did not employ trainers in their display team. the aircraft's Indian Air Force serial reflects that of a genuine IAF MiG-21UM.

Final systems checks and engine/afterburner tests were carried out at Bankstown Airport before the aircraft was transported by road to Sydney's Kingsford-Smith International Airport where the 3962m (13,000ft), Botany Bay runway was considered more appropriate for the MiGs first flight.

Designated pilot for this historic flight was Squadron Leader Phil Frawley, a highly qualified Royal Australian Air Force FA-18 Hornet and Mirage IIIO pilot (and also the designated pilot for the RAAF Museum CA-27 Sabre - see WW's excellent *F-86 Sabre* title in the *Warbirds Today* series). He was accompanied by a European air force pilot with twenty one years experience on the MiG-21.

During the 140 km (76nm), ten minute flight from Sydney to the RAAF's fighter base at Williamtown, the MiG utilised the callsign 'Fishbed Two One' and as part of the flight it was intercepted by two FA-18 Hornets of No.77 Sqn. flown by Flt. Lts. Peter 'Alf' Speiss and Leon 'OD' O'Donohue and was obliged to 'die gracefully' at their hands.

It was gratifying that after such a long and complex rebuild only one snag, the failure of an instrument light bulb, was noted on the first flight. Initial test and pilot familiarisation/training flights were carried out at Williamtown and these proving flights amazed the RAAF by the extremely low maintenance time required per flying hour compared with that of the FA-18. RAAF pilots have also gained a new respect for what could have been a potential adversary.

Sonic Aviation will base the MiG at the Williamtown RAAF Base *Fighter World Museum* from which it will operate for its major air displays and public demonstrations. At the time of writing the aircraft's first public appearance had not been announced but it will undoubtedly be a spectacular addition to Australia's airshow circuit. WW Peter Anderson.

WARBIRDS WORLDWIDE

Let's Get 'em Flying!

MICROSCAN
Engineering

Specialists in CNC and manual machining of warbird parts, particularly for the Spitfire

We can supply parts for any warbird and ship to any part of the world............

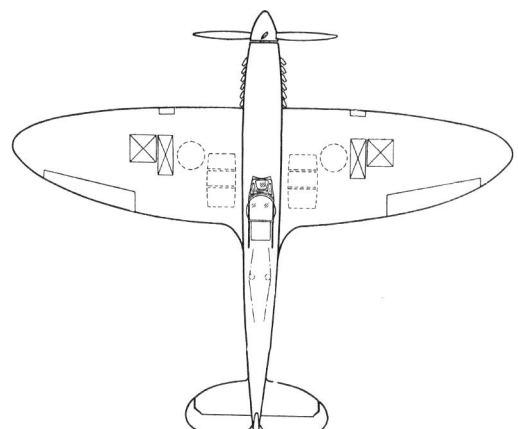

- We are experienced in the machining of awkward and hard to get components for your warbird.

- *Microscan* can make parts to your specifications, using your drawings or an unserviceable or damaged component.

- Let *Microscan Engineering* help to get your Spitfire, Hurricane, Mustang or Axis warbird into the air more quickly.

- Contact Martin Edwards or Glen Richardson for immediate personal attention on (0602) 736588 or Fax (0602) 461557.

Microscan Engineering Limited, Acton Close, Acton Trading Estate, Long Eaton, Nottingham NG10 1FZ England

---

THE WARBIRD INSURANCE SPECIALISTS

EHA
The Essential Link

We already arrange insurance coverage for a growing number of leading European warbird (piston and jet) operators and airshow organisers. We will negotiate with the Insurance Markets top underwriters to provide a policy that is tailored to your exact requirements, at the same time providing a high level of personal service and enthusiasm.

Contact Nigel Foster on 071 739 3709 or Fax 071 613 0546 or at Edgar Hamilton (Aviation) Limited, 69/71 Great Eastern Street LONDON EC2A 3HU and at Lloyd's for an immediate response.

EDGAR HAMILTON AVIATION
A Subsidiary of Edgar Hamilton Limited

Above: M8+ZE sat in the woods in Northern Russia. No camouflage paint remains on the aircraft, the only paint being the fuselage cross and squadron codes. (Kilikow)

Mark Sheppard details the research carried out into the history of Bf110 W.Nr. 4502
Colour Profile by **Terry Lawless**

Bf110 W. Nr. 4502 was recovered from a forested area in Northern Russia in January 1992 and was delivered to Jim Pearce's facility in W.Sussex. Basic stripping down of the airframe was started soon after and thankfully major components such as undercarriage legs and radiators were found to be totally restorable. The two DB601A's were disassembled and found to be in exceptional condition, apart for some corrosion to the head case which of course is inverted on the Daimler Benz 601 engines. More details of the recovery of this airframe can be found in *Warbirds Worldwide 21*. After two years of intensive research by several people we can now reveal more details about the history of this exciting warbird.

In the spring of 1994, the Bf110 E2, code M8+ZE was sold (along with other 110's and Ju87's) to the *Alpine Fighter Collection* in Wanaka, New Zealand. During the last two years, gradually more information has been discovered about the history of this Me110 and a major breakthrough occurred when Norwegian historian Cato Guhnfeldt discovered Gerhard Sarodnik. Cato was researching the history of one of the Norwegian airfields used by the unit JG5. Whilst contacting ex-JG5 members, M8+ZE was discussed and it came to light that Sarodnik was alive and living in the old East Berlin. Thanks to Cato, that we have the story on the operational life of M8+ZE whilst she was at JG5.

Aircraft History.

Research undertaken by Matti Salonen has revealed that this E2 model was one of the final batch of Bf110's produced prior to the proposed switch over to the new Me210. It looks as though it was the 122nd aircraft in a batch of about 153 E2's manufactured at the main Bf110 factory of BFW (*Bayische Fluzeugwerke*) at Augsburg. (This batch of aircraft, W.Nr 4381-4533 were produced there between March 1941 and August 1941), with W.Nr 4502 being completed at the end of July 1941. It was issued with the *Stammkennzeichen* (factory codes) of CD+MV. After air testing it was taken on charge by the Luftwaffe before being delivered to *Geschwaderstab* ZG76, most likely in Stavanger, Norway, marked up as an aircraft of the staff flight, carrying a 'green' aircraft letter Z. (Why the fuselage of W.Nr4502 recovered carried the older W.Nr3084 is still a mystery unless this previous C model and others noted within the same batch were never completed. It is possible that during a factory reorganisation they were instead sidelined and gradually completed over a period of time, later included within other blocks of 110's being manufactured).

The staff unit usually operated with three to six aircraft. During this period (1941) the *Geschwaderstab* was operating with all the Gruppes of ZG76, ie I, II and III, then based in

Red Sailor's
MESSERSCHMITT Bf110

Left: Bf110s being escorted by Bf109Es, both aircraft are from JG5 in 1942/43. The 110 still carries the factory codes of VN+CX. Above: Uffz Emil Gross in the cockpit and Uffz gerhard Sarodnik on the rim - early 1942 (via R. Chapman).

Norway and earmarked for the Defence of the North Sea.

After being allocated a crew, the 110 was operating from Stavanger when the crew made their first 'kill', an RAF aircraft. The date is uncertain though research continues. *Operation Barbarossa* commenced on the 22nd July 1941, but operations in Norway did not commence until the 25th. The four Russian 'kills' were picked up in the weeks commencing with the last 'kill' on the 15th August 1941. Who picked up these kills, either in M8+ZE or another aircraft is unclear. Presently we are trying to identify the pilots who were operating with Stab/ZG76 during this period; this requires further research.

In early 1941, I Gruppe returned to Germany, but 110's of the 2 Staffel stayed in Kirkennes and operated their 110's alongside the aircraft of JG5. In May 1941 the III Gruppe was disbanded, returning to Germany. Finally, in the Autumn the last Gruppe, No. II, disbanded.

With ZG76 no longer existing, the staff flight was in limbo. It is thought that M8+ZE, other aircraft of the staff flight and 2/ZG76 and 110's flying with JG5 operated as an enlarged unit in Northern Norway. It is believed that the staff flight acted as *Jafü*, a command structure co-ordinating all heavy fighter operations in *Luftflotte 5*. It seems likely that M8+ZE possibly stayed with this new enlarged unit for a while before returning to the *Werft* (Maintenance Unit) at Stavanger, where it was used as a familiarisation aircraft for new ZG aircrews. Here it stayed until the 13th February; this is where the main story starts.

50 years on.

Uffz (Unteroffizier) Emil Gross and Uffz Gerhard Sarodnik arrived in Norway to join the *Zerstörer Kette* of JG77 just after *Operation Barbarossa* had started, both from unit ZG26. Here they flew together as a team operating the Bf110 with 1(Z)JG77, undertaking operational missions against Murmansk and bomber escort missions, attacking the convoys being used to supply lend lease materials.

The story really begins on the 7th January 1942. On the day in question, *Rottenführer Fw* (Feldwebel) Weißenburger (later Major with 208 'kills') and his wingman, Uffz Emil Gross (flying in LN+MR) took off from Rovaniemi, departing at 1055hrs. They had been allocated the task of giving cover to two Ju87's who's mission was to attack Russian barracks over Murmansk. On reaching the target, Weißenburger gave the specific order to Gross that they were to circle above the Stuka's during the attack and keep a watch out for Russian fighters. This they duly did and after a two hour escort mission, the 110's returned to Rovaniemi at 1253hrs.

On returning to base, the Stuka pilots bitterly complained of the lack of fighting spirit of their escort. After due consideration the Kommodore of the Stuka unit made an official complaint to JG5 with a request that the crews involved be disciplined. At the hearing at the end of January, the two experienced Bf110 pilots were punished; being 'sentenced' to no operational missions for two weeks because of the accusations levelled at them. They reacted in a resigned way as it was clear to them that their young squadron *Staffelkapitän*, Oblt (Oberleutnant) Felix Brandis (KIA a few days later on the 2nd February), would not risk dealing with it by just giving them a verbal warning; the accusations came from a higher authority.

Still unhappy about the injustice of their punishment, Emil Gross and his radio operator Gerhard Sarodnik eventually joined in the flying again on the 13th February 1942. Due to very few new Bf110's arriving over the previous few months, (largely due to switched production to the failed Me210), the numbers of aircraft remaining operational with the Zerstörer units was becoming painfully low. (Quoted in Luftwaffe strength reports for all *Zerstörergruppen* as 44 available, with 28 being serviceable as of 13th December 1941). By February things were not much better, so when spare aircraft did became available, mostly second hand models, they were col-

lected as soon as possible and delivered to their new unit.

They received orders to take over a spare aircraft which had become available at Stavanger-Forus and take it to Rovaniemi in Northern Finland. The Bf110, located at Stavanger, was already weathered with exhaust stains from previous operational use and still carried the codes of M8+ZE; her first unit, *Geschwaderstab ZG76*.

On the 13th February the ferry flight began, with M8+ZE taking off at 1645hrs from Stavanger-Forus taking routing via Denmark, Germany and Finland. On the 23rd, on the last leg of the journey, they landed at Kiestinki at 1210hrs. Here the handover was undertaken and so W.Nr4502 joined the ranks of 6(Z)JG5, after a total flying time of nearly 10 hours over ten days. (Interestingly, also Bf110 E2's W.Nr4500 CD+MT joined 1(Z)JG77 and were two of the five '110's damaged/lost during the brief six week existence of 6(Z) JG5)

There was however no time for a break and just 25 minutes later, after being refuelled and armed with two SC250kg (550lb) bombs, they were airborne again for their first operational mission. They headed East and bombed a train along the Murman rail route; the main artery for materials delivered on lend lease through to Murmansk and into the rest of Russia, returning to Kiestinki at 1325hrs having destroyed a locomotive. Later, at 1345hrs they were to escort a Fiesler Storch which had successfully recovered the shot down Zerstörer - pilot Oblt Franzisket and his radio operator - from behind enemy lines at Polijarny-Krug. (W.Nr4502's sister ship W.Nr4501), returning and landed at 1450hrs. At 1630hrs they were eventually together with other machines of 6(Z)JG5, heading west to Rovaniemi airfield, landing at 1730hrs.

The Red Sailor.

Up until their next mission, Gross and Sarodnik had a break of a full day in the war which Sarodnik openly criticised with remarks as "Why don't we end the war in the same way as the sailors showed us in 1918". With this derogatory remark, he got himself the nickname of *Der Rote Matrose* (The Red Sailor) by his squadron. (The remark refers to the mutiny in the German Navy at Kiel on the 3rd November 1918 which forced the Kaiser to

Red Sailor's Bf110

abdicate and so end World War I). This would not be the last remark of this nature Sarodnik would make but it is quite strange that none of his comrades felt obliged to denounce him because his remarks (during the reign of the Third Reich) were classed as treasonable. This nickname has stayed with him until this day, more than 50 years after the event!

On the 25th February 1942, Gross and Sarodnik were on an other escort mission with M8+ZE. Taking off at 1020hrs they escorted Ju88's to Kandalakscha, this time landing at Alakurti airstrip at 1147hrs. Later the same day, at 1407hrs they took off to escort some Ju87's to Kandalakscha railway station where they experienced flak. They returned to Rovaniemi at 1545hrs.

On the 26th, the squadron got airborne at 1130hrs and flew to Kirkenes in Norway, providing an escort later that day. They arrived at 1255hrs and were refuelled ready for the mission. At 1604hrs they took off meeting up with the Ju88's en route. The target for the Ju88's was the harbour at Poljarnoje Inlet, where lend lease shipping was anchored. On reaching the target they again experienced flak, but otherwise was an uneventful trip and returned to Kirkenes, landing at 1725hrs. This were the last mission for Gross and Sarodnik for approximately two weeks. Bad weather and extremely low serviceability of the aircraft reduced any missions to an absolute minimum. (A condition which is common during the winter in this part of the world.).

The Final Mission.

In the second week of March, the weather had improved to such an extent that regular missions were possible. On Wednesday the 11th March 1942, Gross and Sarodnik were in the cockpit of M8+ZE (by this time their regular aircraft). The target for the day was the airfield at Murmaschi, on the Murmansk railway, 120 miles(200km) ESE from Kirkenes and approximately due south of Murmansk. Two of the six Bf110's participating in the mission were to attack the airfield at low level in order to prevent the Russian fighters from taking off. The remaining four aircraft, amongst them M8+ZE were to bomb the airfield afterwards from a relatively safe height.

At 1636 Emil Gross in M8+ZE took off from the landing strip at Kirkenes, loaded with two SC250kg (550Ib) bombs fixed below the fuselage, and climbed to join the five aircraft flying up front. Shortly before reaching the target, the four 110's allocated for bombing climbed to height with M8+ZE remaining a little behind. Here they began experiencing flak from the airfield and were surprised by the appearance of a hoard of Russian fighters. The 20+ fighters, a mixture of MiG-1's and lend-lease Hurricanes split up and three of the fighters focused their efforts on the aircraft at the rear, in this case M8+ZE. Seconds later machine gun and cannon fire starting hitting the air-

Uffz Sarodnik in his Bordfunk position whilst with 10(Z)JG5 in 42/43. He was the radio operator/rear gunner (Rick Chapman)

craft from the rear port quarter and Gross jettisoned the bomb load. A 20mm cannon shell went through the port main spar of the tail unit, with 7.62mm calibre bullets penetrating the starboard wing and DB601A. Thick black smoke suddenly appeared from the damaged motor. The second attack came from directly in front; a round hit the armoured windscreen, splintering the armour glass to such an extent that Gross was covered with glass shards. Luckily he was looking sideways and was hit in his cheek, badly rupturing it. Had he been looking straight ahead, he would have been hit directly and would have almost certainly been blinded and possibly killed.

After a cry for help, Emil Gross could just about compose himself sufficiently to attempt a crash landing. The low starboard wing, which had dropped due to the damaged engine and the temporary loss of concentration from the injury, was raised. With the Bf110 only 400 feet above the ground, the two crew members quickly realised the machine was too badly hit to stay in the air for much longer. Whilst Gross tried to keep the Bf110 under control, Sarodnik succeeded in firing off a red distress flare from the rear cockpit in the hope that it would be noticed by one of the other crews. Despite his tremendous pain, Emil Gross tried to belly land M8+ZE on a lightly upward slopping hill. The Bf110 bounced and slid on the deep snow, cutting a swath through small trees, gradually losing speed until it came to a halt within a clump of trees near the summit. Coming to a stop, the outer three metres of starboard wing was severed by a tree, causing it to crash onto the rear cockpit and narrowly missing Sarodnik. Within seconds Gross and Sarodnik were out of the aircraft and laying face down in the snow, expecting to hear an almighty detonation. However, everything around remained silent.

A night in the wilderness.

Only 24 minutes had elapsed since the take off. It was 1720. Gross, with his open and heavily bleeding face injury, was in a bad state. He asked Sarodnik to shoot him as he could not see the possibility of surviving the long walk through enemy territory in an extremely cold and snow covered landscape back to German lines. Leaving him behind would have meant he would have been taken prisoner by the Russians. He wanted to avoid this under any circumstances, even if the price for it had to be his life. In the crash, Sarodnik was only slightly injured and he steadfastly refused to shoot his partner, eventually convincing Gross they should find a hide out before darkness set in. They went back to the aircraft and removed snow boots, sleeping bags and food, along with the emergency kit and their parachutes. They managed to find a hollow in the roots of a tree located above a suitable recess, approximately half a kilometre away from the aircraft. They then used the parachutes to make this into their temporary shelter. Afterwards Sarodnik attended to Emil Gross's face injury as best he could. Darkness fell as did the temperature, to minus 40 degrees C and they estimated their chances of survival were as bleak as the polar night outside. The one good thing they did not have to worry about that night, considering their location in the middle of nowhere and so far behind enemy lines, was enemy troops. They did have one visitor though, a bear; to their relief it left quite quickly.

Rescue

What they did not know however was that the red distress flare which Sarodnik had fired had been seen by one of the other crews and the preparation for rescuing them the following morning was already underway.

It had in fact been a bad day, for not only losing W.Nr. 4502 as a 100% loss, two other 110's had to undertake emergency landings at Kirkenes after this chase; Bf110 E2 W Nr 2651 suffered 90% damage and the other sister ship Bf110 E2 W.Nr. 4500 suffered 70% damage. 6(Z) JG5 suffered 50% losses on their 11th March operation.

Early in the morning, Gross and Sarodnik left their hideout and started to travel westwards towards home. Gross in particular found walking difficult; apart from his general injuries, his right foot was seriously frost-bitten. They were not successful in binding together Gross's right flying boot sufficiently enough to keep the snow out. (Another bullet went through the side of the cockpit at floor level and this is thought to have split the heel of Gross's right boot). After walking several kilometres through deep snow and patchy forest, they heard the noise of an aircraft. They quickly recognised that the aircraft belonged to their own squadron. Sarodnik fired a flare and minutes later the Bf110 (being flown by *Staffelkapitän* Oblt Karl-Freidrich Schloßtein) circled above them.

The aircraft slowed down and waggled its wings, indicating to them the direction of a suitable landing strip. Both knew now that their rescuers would soon be on their way. Shortly after 1600hrs a Storch landed, transporting them to safety of the Kirkenes airfield. (Sarodnik even recorded this flight in his log book!) This was not the only time Sarodnik was forced to crash land behind enemy lines - it happened again two years later but that's another story.

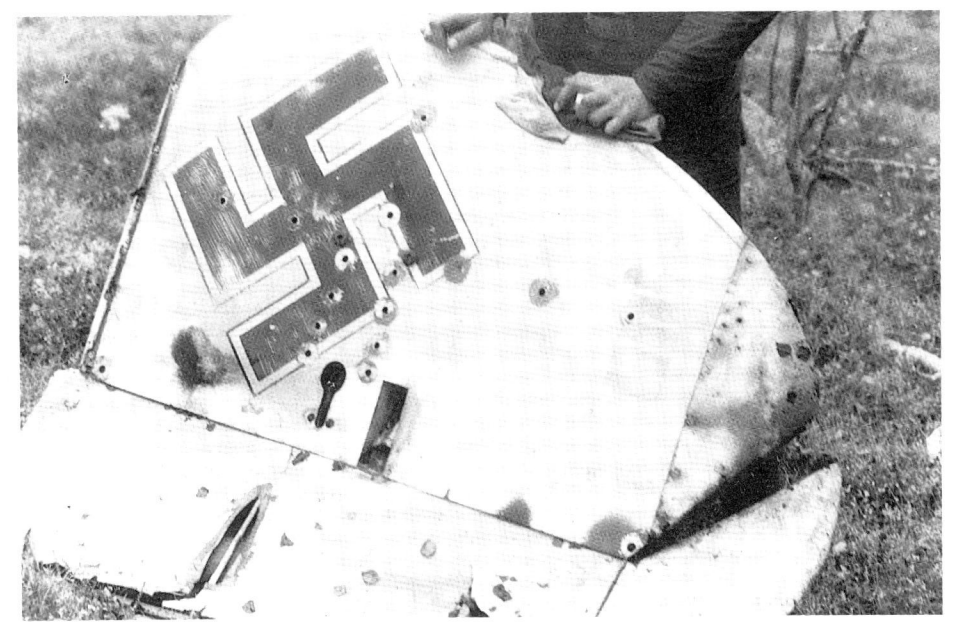

At this point the relationship of the two flyers ended, as did the active life of Bf110 E2 CD+MV, W.Nr 4502, and M8+ZE of 6(Zerstörer staffel) Jagdgeschwader 5 'Eismeer'. It was listed as a 100% loss in the Luftwaffe Quartermasters returns for 11th March 1942 and sat in a deep sleep within the forest for 50 years until recovery.

Recuperation.

After a stay in a Luftwaffe recuperation hospital home in Italy and home leave in Germany, Gerhard Sarodnik returned to 10(Z) and later 13(Z)JG5, where he served until the end of the war.

As a result of the severe frostbite suffered by Emil Gross, part of his right foot had to be amputated and he was transferred for treatment to a military hospital in Germany. He is said to have seen the end of the war as a Ju52 pilot. After the war he returned to his home town of Graz in Austria where he worked as an electrician, as he did before the war broke out. Unfortunately Gross has not been heard from since the end of the war, but it is hoped that he or his family will be located in the near future and if anybody can help it would be most appreciated.

The Mystery Unit 6(Z)JG5.

It was always believed that M8+ZE belonged to 10(Z)JG5 when she was lost. The Luftwaffe quartermasters returns showed it as belonging to 6(Z)JG5 which for a long time was thought to be an error, especially as the more detailed loss reports states it belonged to 10(Z)JG5. The mystery of 6(Z) was discussed with author Werner Girbig, an expert on JG5 and a number of surviving crew members from JG5. The question was always asked, did you ever belong to this unit? The answer was always no; the only units they were members of were 10(Z) and later 13(Z)JG5. The breakthrough came via correspondence between two ex-members of JG5, radio operator Lt Gerhard Freidrich and pilot Oblt Karl-Freidrich Schloßtein. In the mid 1980's it was stated that his Luftwaffe *Wehrpass* (Officers pass etc), confirmed he had belonged to the *6 Zerstörer Staffeln*. The unit only existed for six weeks from the beginning of February 1942 until 16th March 1942 and it seems only a few crew members had this stamped into their documents. (Which is possibly why none of the surviving pilots of JG5 have any recollections of this unit ever existing!) Also nearly all the crew members who were still with JG5 at the end of the war had all their log books and ID records confiscated by the British troops; they were no doubt burned.

From the records then, it looks as though W.Nr4502 and her sister W.Nr4501 were the only losses for the 6(Z)staffeln during that six weeks. Why the 1(Z)JG77 became 6(Z)JG5, the *6 Staffeln* being part of the II Gruppe JG5 is a mystery. The II Gruppe became fully operational in May 1942 incorporating Jagdgruppe Zbv flying Bf109's. It is possible that they were going to include the Zerstörer unit within the II Gruppe to become a mixed unit. After this short period the policy possibly changed and later the I, II, and III Gruppes all became single engine fighter units with the Z staffel becoming a separate unit within JG5. **WW Mark Sheppard.**

Thanks must go to Sir Tim Wallis of the *Alpine Fighter Collection* for his help, Cato Guhnfeldt for locating Gerhard Sarodnik; Rick Chapman, Hannu Valtonen, Matti Salonen and Michael Freidrich for their help in compiling this article and to Siegfried Angerer in Austria for helping me to try and locate Emil Gross.

COLOUR PROFILE PAGE 43

Top: *The remains of the port fin showing the five black bars indicating 'kills', one RAF roundel and four Russian stars.* ***Below:*** *This shot shows how remarkably complete the 110 is. Though there appears to be many missing panels these were recovered with the aircraft.*

FOR SALE
Cessna A-37B Dragonfly

Cessna A37B Dragonfly - Four complete aircraft with history plus spares package, available individually. Located in Australia - opportunity to own SAFE modern RELIABLE twin engine jet with unbelievable acceleration and performance that you can operate from your local field

Enquires to:
Australian Aviation Facilities Pty Ltd
Phone 61-2-7910200 Fax 61-2-7910325

THE BOOMERANG STORY

Australian Produced

VIDEO

FINALLY A FULL 47 MINUTE DOCUMENTARY ON THE BOOMERANG AIRCRAFT

FEATURING:
- Full history.
- Spectacular flying action of the only airworthy Boomerang today.
- Never released file footage.
- Interviews with WW2 Boomerang pilots.
- Featuring Boomerang restoration.
- Location Footage on Boomerang Operations.

This is a spectacular and informative documentary on the most significant aircraft in Australian Aviation history.

Place your order now and send to: Nomad Television Productions, P.O. Box 112 Darling Heights, QLD-4350, Australia or Fax: 076/ 300229

A$39.95 Plus P&P; add A$5.00 for PAL and A$10.00 for NTSC
Send Cheque or Money Order or
Bankcard/Visa/Mastercard No. and expiry date

FOR SALE

Rolls-Royce
GRIFFON V-12
Aero Engines

Brand New Nil Hours
Inhibited and Sealed in transit boxes
at £7500.00 each o.n.o.

Also Marinised Griffon V12 Nil Hours
+ Prop & Issota Fraschini W18 cyl
New In Stand

Phone 0257 463198
or Fax 0257 464246 (UK)

Messerschmitt Bf110 E2 Zerstorer W.Nr.4502

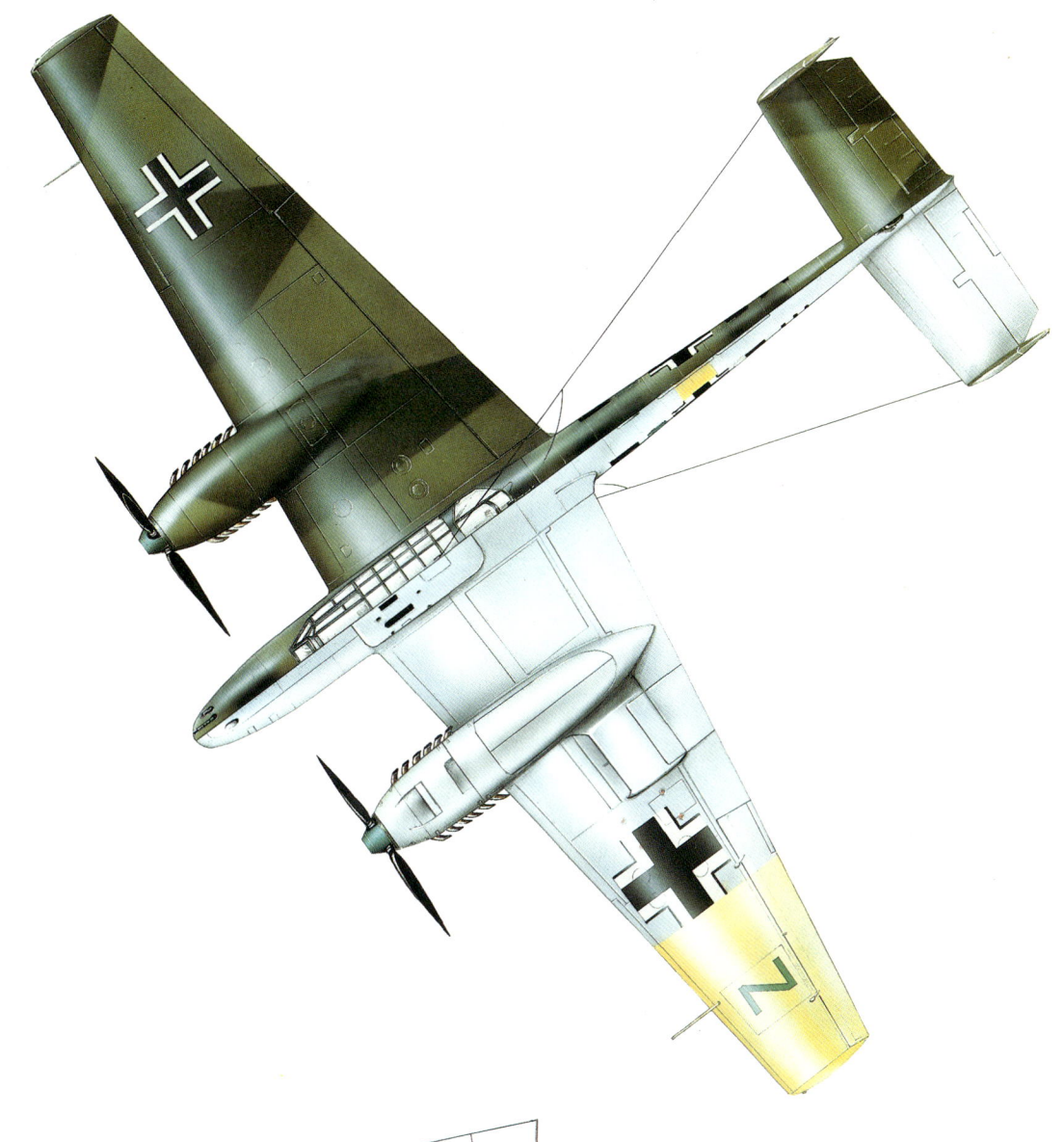

Bf110 E2 W. Nr.4502. Manufactured July 1941 with factory codes CD+MV. Issued to Stab ZG76. Transferred to 6(Z)/JG5 23.2.42. Shot down by fighters 11.3.42. Artwork strictly copyright Warbirds Worldwide and Terry Lawless 1994.

Hawker Fury - in the minds of the warbird industry this name conjures up the image of the ultimate big piston fighter - an aircraft competing with the Grumman Bearcat for the title 'Ultimate Piston engined Warbird'. In its heyday of operational capability with the Royal Navy the Sea Fury represented a highly developed and sophisticated high performance piston aircraft. It presented pilots with the opportunity to fly perhaps the highest performance single engined piston aircraft ever built for military operations.

Today a number of these superb aircraft survive in civilian hands and are now a much revered Warbird - an aircraft which has achieved both a fearsome reputation as an Unlimited Racer and also a reputation as a desirable - if expensive - high performance private sport plane. This feature details the background behind one particular Englishman's desire to own and operate one

Hawker FURY

of these magnificent aircraft as a private venture. I hope in some small way here to portray not just the enormous expense involved for any private individual contemplating such a venture but also the commitment in both time and skill that is required to properly satisfy all the operational, engineering and safety requirements that make up a professionally constituted warbird operation.

John Bradshaw is a remarkable man, perhaps typical of the early breed of RAF professional airmen who clearly believe in excelling at everything he does. John has had a long and varied career in both military flying in the Royal Air Force and in civilian airline operations and this report centres on his own personal desire to own and operate a high performance piston engined warbird.

John is an ex Halton 'Brat', having trained as an Aircraft Engineer at the RAF's No.1 School of Technical Training from 1947 to 1950. He is proud of the fact that having been a Halton prize winner he is now one of the few people still actively involved in aviation who has shaken the hand of "Boom Trenchard" father of the Royal Air Force. Having graduated at Halton John went on to pilot training with the RAF on Chipmunks and Airspeed Oxfords during the early 1950's and, following completion of his aircrew training, was posted to an operational ground attack Squadron - No 145 Sqn 2nd TAF - flying Vampires and Venoms in Germany, in 1953. During the subsequent

Opposite Page: *N36SF with John Bradshaw at the controls. The paint scheme is not only high quality but unique in that it portrays the national insignia of the air arms that operated the type.*

John Bradshaw climbing into the neat cockpit of the ex Iraqi Hawker Fury N36SF prior to a training flight.

Richard Paver interviews **John Bradshaw** and gets an insight into operating Hawkers' thoroughbred Fury.
Photography by the author.

three years he became the highest scoring pilot on the wing and also formed and led the unit formation aerobatic team.

Following completion of this operational tour in 1956 he was posted to the Central Flying School at Swinderby to become an instructor on Vampires. A year later he resigned his commission to join what was then BOAC - later to become British Airways - flying DC-7s, VC10s and ultimately Concorde. During these pioneering years on Concorde John established world speed records between New York - London (2hrs 56 mins) and Miami - London (3hrs 49 mins.) In a 28 year career with the company he served on Concorde from 1977 to 1985 retiring as a senior Concorde Captain in 1985, thus completing a period of flying which he describes as 'the highlight of his career in the most superb airliner ever built'.

Having retired from BA John didn't have any desire to take things easy. He took on a new job flying Jet Provosts for the RAF as a civilian at the Central Air Traffic Control School at Shawbury - John describes this role as an airborne "Mouse" acting as a stooge for the School to practice air traffic control on him. He then 'retired' again but subsequently came back as an RAF reserve Officer instructing full time on Bulldogs between May 1990 and 1993.

During the final years of his career with BA John's mind turned to his retirement ambitions and amongst others these included a desire to own a decent car after driving old bangars from "thiefrow" airport and an ambition to attend the National Championship Air Races at Reno. The ambition to attend Reno was satisfied in 1986 when he and his wife Barbara spent a week at the Reno Air Races. Fascinated with the power and spectacle of the 'worlds fastest motor sport' he and Barbara have now attended annually since then. However it was the 1986 races that set off another ambition in his mind - that was an overwhelming desire to own and fly a Hawker Sea Fury.

I recently asked John why he got into Sea Fury flying. He replied that his interest origi-

Hawker Fury

nated from seeing a number of them competing so well at Reno in 1986 - where thoroughbred British Naval Fighters took Gold in the home of U.S. National Championship Air Racing against stiff competition. The Fury looked good both in the air and on the ground. From that moment on John harboured an ambition to fly a Fury and the next year put the word out that he was on the lookout to purchase a decent airworthy example.

This was to lead him on a trail of assessing a number of Furies for possible acquisition - both projects and existing airworthy aircraft. A couple of years were spent during the late 1980s flying back and forth between the U.K. and U.S. checking out a number of the type. It must be emphasised at this point that the Sea Fury was not exactly readily available, despite the efforts of a number of U.S. restorers and for a couple of years Johns choice was limited to two particular examples; one of which was available in California and one on the market in Chicago. Being a fully qualified engineer John was quite selective in his choice. His objective was to secure a basically sound flyable stock airframe/engine combination which could be brought up to a high standard of both technical and aesthetic excellence once it was returned to the U.K. In 1990 John was made aware of an Ex Iraqi Fury under rebuild to fly at the *Coleman Museum* in Texas which was being advertised as available for sale following restoration. He immediately contacted Kenny Day at Coleman and arranged to fly out to Texas with his wife to inspect the aircraft. At the time of his inspection the Fury was nearing completion - it had first been ground run in August 1989 - and when John saw it his first impressions were favourable.

The aircraft - N36SF - was one of a large batch acquired by David Tallichet and Ed Jurist from

The Fury crew (L to R): Dave Lloyd, John Duncan, John Bradshaw, Ron Collins, Jerry Bull, Tony Miles, James Gregory.

the Iraqi Air Force in 1979 - 28 Furies had been discovered in the 1970s in Iraq and following a series of complex negotiations were subsequently shipped to Florida. N36SF had been sold by Jurist and Tallichet and ended up at the *Coleman Museum* in the late 1980s where Kenny Day set about its restoration.

Though it has been popularly reported that the Jurist and Tallichet Furies were acquired in a derelict condition having been in open storage in the desert for many years - John Bradshaw is not totally convinced that this is completely true, as his example had been very well preserved with a fully inhibited engine and may well have come out of covered storage in Iraq.

When John arrived at the *Coleman Museum* to check out this particular Fury in 1990 he was greeted with the sight of an almost complete machine in an overall white primer paint scheme. He immediately set about carrying out a detailed survey to assess its condition. After the survey, which took some two days, John decided the aircraft was a basically sound example and set about negotiating its purchase. A deal was eventually struck over a breakfast meeting with the *Coleman Museum* on August 2nd 1990.

This date is indelibly imprinted on Johns memory because on that particular day he had been unable to purchase his customary newspaper to check out the exchange rates before the early morning meeting and only after agreeing a deal did he discover the breakout that same day of the Gulf War which sent all the Western economies and exchange rates into immediate turmoil. Johns immediate thoughts were that the time was not right to be contemplating the purchase of a Fury as the Western economies were likely to be affected and fuel prices increased - however he was not prepared to renege on a handshake and so went ahead and completed the purchase.

The reward for John was that he had purchased a basically sound aeroplane, overhauled at the *Coleman Museum* over a period of two years. Whilst it was accepted that the Coleman Museum had not set out to create a *Concours d'elegance* example the aeroplane was nonetheless sound and in both airframe and engine hours relatively young.

At this stage, as John was still employed by the Royal Air Force instructing on Bulldogs and had to return immediately to the U.K., it was some months later in Easter 1991 before he was able to return to Coleman for his initial training and check out in the Fury. In the meantime Kenny Day had finished the restoration in Texas and repainted the aircraft in Johns chosen colour scheme. This scheme (which the Fury still wears) was the joint first choice of both John and his wife Barbara as they both had been very taken by a Royal Australian Navy scheme which they had first seen on one of the aircraft they had inspected earlier.

John contracted the *Coleman Museum* to spray the Fury in a deep blue metallic overall, similar to that worn by the Australian Navy Aerobatic team; the only variation being that the aircraft was adorned with four different sets of roundels to represent the major air arms which operated the type. The aircraft now wears an Australian fuselage roundel on the starboard side, a Dutch Air Force roundel on the port fuselage side, British roundels on the wing top surfaces and Canadian roundels on the wing undersides. The paint finish is superb with the colours looking quite different from varying angles according to the fall of the light. The paint is a one process metallic polyurethane paint, not a solid paint with lacquer.

During Easter 1991 John and Barbara, accompanied by Engineer Ron Collins, returned to Texas. Ron was in the Royal Navy during the early 'fifties and had extensive experience with Sea Furies during the Korean War. His remarkable technical memory of was to prove invaluable.

John explained that prior to returning to Texas he had spent a great deal of time in the UK researching as much as possible about Fury flight operations. After reading all the flight manuals he spent a lot of time discussing the flight characteristics of the Fury with experienced Fury pilots in both the U.S.A. and U.K. He had approached the subject in a totally professional manner and was committed to flying

Below: *John Bradshaw taxies out at Benson prior to a training flight*

Let's Get'em Flying!

the aircraft with the best possible preparation and training. He already had extensive tail-wheel experience included in his 17,000 hours flying time on aircraft such as the Mosquito, Spitfire and Provost.

Initially John carried out high and low speed taxi trials at Coleman Airfield. However the runway there was only just within limits, being only 3200 ft long - and the paved area was rather narrow.

John concluded that on his first flight he would take the Fury to nearby Brownwood, Texas, approximately 30 miles from Coleman. The runway at Brownwood was both wider and longer.

Prior to undertaking his first Fury flight John had been through a thorough check out with Howard Pardue at Breckenridge. Whilst Howard was happy to sign out John the Federal Aviation Administration insisted that they issue a letter of pilot authorisation directly themselves. The FAA agreed to provide an examiner to be present at Brownwood on the day of John's planned first flight, when a full check examination would take place.

The day (Easter 1991) duly arrived when John was ready to fly the Fury. He approached his first flight with considerable trepidation. These feelings were enhanced by the fact that this particular Fury had been rarely flown since completion of the overhaul, and it had previously (in the hands of the *Coleman Museum*) suffered electrical problems on take off, resulting in an aborted launch and overrun of the runway. These two factors combined with the short narrow runway at Coleman and John's lack of experience on type led to a situation which had to be treated with the greatest respect.

In the event the first take off - in his words - "went like a dream" - and all the preparation paid off as he successfully flew the aircraft to Brownwood 30 miles away, landing in full view of the waiting FAA examiner. John taxied to the Brownwood ramp where the examiner signalled to him, holding up three fingers signifying he wanted to see three full stop landings and take offs there and then in front of him.

The day was scorching hot, and despite sweltering under the intense heat of the perspex canopy and with little time to collect his thoughts, John deftly turned the Fury round and set off to carry out his check ride pattern of three take offs and full stop landings.

These were duly flown for the FAA. But the requirement for consecutive full stop landings resulted in the brakes getting rather warm and so after each take off John deliberately left the undercarriage down for an extended period in order to get some cooling air flow around the wheels. The Fury handbook advises against extended circuit work as the engine oil temperature can rise beyond limits; the lack of airspeed inhibiting the Oil cooler from operating effectively.

After performing his check flight John was relieved to land for the fourth time that day at Brownwood and put the aircraft to bed for the night. On completion of the checkout the FAA examiner rewarded John with a letter of authority for the Fury.

The next day dawned hot and still, and John intending to start immediately on his formal work up training to display standard in the aircraft. Once again he took off from Brownwood for a standard follow up training sortie. A few minutes after getting airborne on this second day his knowledge of the Fury emergency drills was to be thoroughly tested. The drive to the auxiliary gearbox failed in flight, leading to the loss of all primary services; hydraulics, electrics and pneumatics. An immediate precautionary landing was made and the aircraft was then towed into the hangar, thankfully in an undamaged state.

The cause of the problem was failure of the shaft coupling to the gearbox drive, and so at midday on a Friday John was left with a dead Sea Fury in the middle of Texas - over 6,000 miles from home with the pressing need to return to the U.K. for business reasons. John then telephoned as many of his U.S. aviation contacts as he could in an attempt to track down a replacement shaft coupling. After many dozens of phone calls he made contact with Craig Charleston in California who saved the day by cheerfully declaring that he had two "new" Centaurus Shaft couplings on the bench in front of him. Craig readily agreed to send one of these off immediately to Brownwood by *Federal Express* and at approximately 5:00 pm on the Friday evening he dispatched the parts. To Johns relief they were duly delivered by air to Brownwood at precisely 7:00 am the next day.

Saturday was spent fitting the new coupling with both John and Ron Collins working on the aircraft and so by that evening the Fury

Top: The Fury at Coleman in 1990 - in white primer. Above: Off loading the aircraft at Southampton - back on English soil at last! (John Bradshaw photographs)

Continued on Page 54

Making the Movie

ATTACK! ATTACK! ATTACK!

THE FANTASTIC STORY BEHIND THE RAID THAT COULD WIN A WAR — OR LOSE A WORLD!

633 SQUADRON

THE MIRISCH CORPORATION presents CLIFF ROBERTSON · GEORGE CHAKIRIS in "633 SQUADRON" co-starring MARIA PERSCHY · HARRY ANDREWS · DONALD HOUSTON Colour by TECHNICOLOR® PANAVISION
Directed by WALTER E. GRAUMAN · Screenplay by JAMES CLAVELL and HOWARD KOCH · Executive Producer LEWIS J. RACHMIL · Produced by CECIL F. FORD

In 1963 the *Mirisch Corporation* began actual production of *633 Squadron* for release through the distributor *United Artists*. The film screenplay had been adapted from the best selling Frederick E. Smith novel of the same name, which was first published in 1956. The book told the story of a fictional but elite squadron, formed to carry out a near impossible mission: to attack a solid fuel factory located at the end of a heavily defended Norwegian fjord - code named *Operation Vesuvius*. For the film various other improbable factors add to make the story more dramatic, the screenplay was written by Howard Kotch and James Clavell who latterly went on to write the immensely successful *Shogun*.

The 'Sixties were very much a boom time for the producers of war films with countless productions under way around the world, confident in the knowledge that the films would most probably be a success at the box office. It was not until the time of the conflict in Vietnam, and the strong anti war feelings which prevailed during that period that the war movie fell out of favour with the cinema going public. Even today in 1994 a war film is considered something of a risky proposition.

It was July 1963 when *633 Squadron* began to become a reality. The second film production unit, led by Roy Stevens and located to RAF Bovingdon aerodrome in Hertfordshire, was at the time home to the Southern Communications Squadron operating Avro Ansons and Percival Pembrokes. The first Mosquito, RS715 arrived by road on July 3rd from Exeter where all the Mosquitoes were obtained. The production of *633 Squadron* would never have been possible if it were not for the fact that No.3 Civilian Anti-Aircraft Co-operation (CAACU) still operated a number of Mosquitoes (TT.35 and T.III marks) on target towing duties and for testing ground based radar defences, on contract to the Ministry of Defence.

Mirisch Corporation hired Group Captain Thomas Gilbert 'Hamish' Mahaddie, DSO, DFC, AFC, CZMC, C.Eng., FRAes, RAF (ret'd). to act as Chief Technical adviser to the production. Hamish purchased a number of the Mosquitoes on behalf of *Mirisch* and was tasked with negotiating to secure the hire of several others via John Crewdson of *Film Aviation Services* (who was responsible for aircrew and

WARBIRDS WORLDWIDE
TWENTY NINE

for co-ordinating the flying sequences), from the RAF, Imperial War Museum and the Skyfame Museum, which was due to open later in the year at Staverton, Gloucestershire. With the retirement of the Mosquitoes from CAACU operations on the 9th May 1963, it was planned that the aircraft would go directly to Bovingdon for commencement of filming. However, during May many of the Mosquitoes left Exeter with most of the aircraft going to 27 MU(Maintenance Unit) at Shawbury, although T.III serial TW117 went to Henlow for the then embryonic RAF Museum. Mosquito serial TA639, left Exeter on June 6th for its new home with the Central Flying School at RAF Little Rissington, where it was stripped of its target towing equipment and repainted in readiness for a planned career as a display aircraft. The colours were to be very short-lived as it duly arrived at Bovingdon on July 15th via Dishforth, on loan to the *Mirisch Corporation*. The Mosquitoes that were unable to fly were roaded in to act as set dressing in either static or taxiable condition. (see listing).

Throughout July Mosquitoes arrived at Bovingdon. They were rapidly readied for their starring role, the target towing equipment was removed and a coat of grey/green camouflage replaced the overall silver paint work, the obvious differences between the TT./B.Mk 35 and T. IIIs available to the pro-

In 1994 there are only two de Havilland Mosquitoes airworthy. *Gary Brown* takes a look back to the sixties and examines the filming of *633 Squadron* and its sequel *Mosquito Squadron*.

and B. IV versions in appearance. The code letters HT- were chosen, which were never worn by Mosquitoes and in the main serials in the HJ... and HR... blocks (although MM398 was observed on T.III TV959 and RF580 adorned RS712 at one stage) were used. During the filming codes and serials were constantly changed. For example on one occasion three Mosquitoes each coded HT-G could be seen at Bovingdon. Differing letters were sometimes carried on the port and starboard sides of fuselage, a continuity department's worst nightmare!

Although the Mosquitoes are the stars of the film as far as aviation enthusiasts are concerned, a few star actors were brought into the production. With a relatively large budget it was important that the film would do well internationally, with a special emphasis on the United States market. To help attract American interest in the film, Cliff Robertson was to assume top billing as Wing Commander Roy Grant, a former Eagle Squadron volunteer, along with the then 'teen idol' George Chakiris who played Lieutenant Erik Bergman of the Norwegian 'Linge' Resistance, ably supported by a wealth of quality British character actors including Harry Andrews.

Whilst preparations were being carried out at Bovingdon the genuine aircrew, led by Captain John Crewdson of *Film Aviation Services*, (who had previously flown spectacular low level sequences for the film *The War Lover*) were being readied for the production at Exeter. Mosquito T.III TW117 was used to convert pilots onto type, although occasionally B.35 TA719 was utilised. CAACU pilot Harry Ellis was tasked with evaluating the pilots for the film, and with only a limited time available (only two flying hours per candidate could be spared on familiarisation) many competent pilots were passed over due to not having flown a comparable type. The final selection consisted of: Captain John Crewdson *(Film Aviation Services)*, Flt. Lt. John 'Jeff' Hawke (RAF), Sqn. Ldr. Graham 'Taffy' Rich (RAF ret'd.), Captain Peter Warden, and Flt. Lt. Chick Kirkham (RAF).

A North American B-25J Mitchell (N9089Z) was used as the flying camera platform, flown by Gregg Board and Martin Caidin. The Mitchell had flown for the filming of *War Lover* the previous year, which had also used Bovingdon as its main base. The B-25, wearing very pseudo RAF markings, actually appears in the final film as a transport aircraft, dropping Bergmann (George Chakiris) into Norway.

Finally with all pre-production complete the filming began late in July 1963. Director Walter

Opposite Page: *633 Squadron Film Poster (BFI Stills)* **Lower:** *TA719 at Bovingdon for the filming of 633 Squadron (R.W. Cranham)* **Above:** *The sad sight of Mosquito RS718 (masquerading as HJ898, HT-G) complete with 'battle damage' at Bovingdon for the filming of 633 Squadron - the Mirisch Corporation film (R.W. Cranham).*

633 Squadron

Top: *Stirring Stuff! Wing Commander Roy Grant (Cliff Robertson) brings his plane back from the raid on Gestapo H.Q. His Navigator Bissel (Scot Finch) is hurt, though from this still it looks more like he is taking a nap (Mirisch Films Ltd. via Skyfame)*

E. Grauman finally called 'Action' and the wide screen format 'Panavision' cameras began to roll. Loch Morar on the west coast of Scotland doubled for the Norwegian fjord, its rocky relief meeting the productions' requirements. Two Mosquitoes - RS709 and RS712 - left Bovingdon on August 15th and positioned at Dalcross (Inverness Airport) to film the attack sequences. Mosquito TA719, on loan from the Skyfame Collection to *Film Aviation Services*, followed on a day later. The RAF owned aircraft were not allowed to participate in this section of the filming, as it was considered too hazardous! TA719 was re-engined with two zero time Merlins to help it successfully carry out the more dramatic, near vertical passes near the cliff face which the production crew was calling for. In the final cut, some model work has been incorporated into the sequence, but this does not overly detract from the excellent low level flying carried out by the air crews, in particular TA719. While filming in Scotland TA719 was due to briefly visit Staverton for the official opening ceremony of the Skyfame Museum (on the 31st August). TA719 failed to make the appointment and a very angry Peter Thomas (founder of Skyfame, and a leading light in the then embryonic aircraft preservation movement) promptly sent a telegram to *Mirisch* in London grounding the aircraft until an agreement could be reached regarding the aircraft's failure to attend the opening. *Mirisch* had not realised that Skyfame were not receiving any financial rewards for TA719's part in the filming. During this time the aircraft was flown back to Bovingdon by Peter Warden. With filming in Scotland severely disrupted for over a week, costing *Mirisch* in the region of £6000 a day, a settlement was hastily found, after a meeting between Peter Thomas and Robert Relyea of *Mirisch*. Certain conditions had to be implemented if TA719 was to continue to be used in the filming, as follows:

1. TA719 would only be flown by Captain Peter Warden. 2. The aircraft would be cleaned and repainted on completion of filming in the colours of 613 Sqn County of Manchester. 3. Skyfame would receive £2000 compensation for the non attendance of TA719 at the opening.

The second unit, 'Aerial', resumed filming during the first week in September to tidy up the remaining loose ends, including some flying out over the Wash (on the East coast of England), before the weather deteriorated with the onset of Autumn. On of these flights 'Jeff' Hawke, flying as red leader of *Champagne Flight* led a formation of three Mosquitoes behind the B-25 camera ship out over the Norfolk coast - the cameras were trying to capture some formation shots over land in Vic and Echelon configuration. At a height of 4500 feet some quarter attacks were made on the Mitchell. After these were completed the B-25 led the formation down over the North Sea to heights as low as 50 ft. After an hour of filming, fuel reserves necessitated a return to Bovingdon. Whilst following the B-25, Hawke suspected its course to be incorrect and broke away leading the Mosquitoes back to Bovingdon, whilst the B-25 headed off in a totally different direction, eventually ending up over Dover!

Meanwhile at Bovingdon, ground scenes were being filmed, including several crash sequences. This has led, in later years, to the film gaining a bad reputation amongst aircraft enthusiasts. Mosquito serial TA642 (coded HT-G) was scheduled to have a very dramatic undercarriage collapse whilst on its landing run, but unfortunately it happened for real on the 1st August, before the scene was due to be filmed. RS718 was now selected to carry out the task on August 9th, also coded HT-G. Before the scene was shot Captain Crewdson inflicted suitable 'battle damage' to give the impression that the aircraft was returning to base in a severely shot up condition. Crewdson taxied the aircraft and then veered off the runway onto the grass at considerable speed with smoke billowing out from the canisters attached to the underside of the fuselage. At the scheduled moment the undercarriage retraction lever was selected up and the aircraft collapsed onto its belly and slewed to a

Above: *The formation flying was very close indeed! RS709 flown by Dizzy Addicott during the flying for Mosquito Squadron (via Peter Thomas, Skyfame).*

halt before the cameras. RS718 was later burnt out for another scene in the film

The demise of TA724 on August 10th, was planned to be even more dramatic. Coded HT-B, the Mosquito was scheduled to collide with a fuel bowser after being shot up by a pair of Bf 109's (actually French Nord's) during its take off run. To achieve this scene, which was considered far too dangerous for the aircraft to be piloted, two sets of wires were attached to a tow bar fastened to the tail wheel. One set

WARBIRDS WORLDWIDE
TWENTY NINE
50

went to the brakes and one set controlled the ignition cut outs. As the aircraft approached the bowser an engineer on the tow bar shut down the power and the Mosquito hit the bowser resulting in an explosion and a tremendous fire. Needless to say it sounded fine in theory but in reality it took three attempts to hit the bowser! During the airfield strafing attack, if you look carefully a silver CAACU marked Mosquito can be seen undergoing maintenance. Additionally, during several take off scenes the resident RAF Southern Communications Squadron Ansons are clearly visible in their white and silver markings. Another misleading cinematic trick with locations occurred while filming Mosquitoes overflying the pub the pilots used to frequent, *The Black Swan*. The audience is given the impression that the pub is just outside the airfield boundary. In reality the pub (called the *Three Compasses Inn*) is actually near Elstree aerodrome at Patchetts Green nearly 10 miles away. Incidentally the exterior of the building is virtually unchanged and is well worth a visit!

Filming was completed in the first two weeks of September and the second 'Aerial' unit returned from Dalcross in Scotland, with the three Mosquitoes flying directly to Biggin Hill in Kent for the first ever *International Air Fair* on September 14th. After being very well received at the display the Mosquitoes went their separate ways back to their owners. The inimitable John 'Jeff' Hawke had gained special permission from *Mirisch* to borrow RS709, so that he could fly back to Wattisham for his demob party. On leaving Biggin Hill Hawke performed one of his renowned low passes before pulling up into a barrel roll; the event is still talked about today, over thirty years later. Following the end of filming *Mirisch* held on to two Mosquitoes, RS712 and RS709 for future use. TA719 was flown back to Staverton by David Ogilvy for display at the Skyfame Museum and the two RAF aircraft, TA639 and TW117 went to Little Rissington and Henlow respectively. After editing, the film was released with an 'A' Certificate on the 23rd August 1964, with a specially composed, stirring martial soundtrack by Ron Goodwin. The film went on to be a success, well received by audiences, although the acting and the script does look very wooden 30 years on. Despite this when the film is shown it still attracts healthy ratings. The professional film critics of the day said;

(Leonard Moaley, *Daily Express* 4th June 64). "The dialogue is so embarrassingly bad, so full of old fashioned heroics that you laugh out loud when you're meant to be weeping qui-

Top: TA719 post 633 Squadron filming coded SY-G (Skyfame). Below: TA639 being refuelled at Bovingdon (MAP).

etly. But the spectacle is a smash hit." (Ann Pagey, *Daily Herald* 5th June 64) "......but the flying sequences are amongst the most exciting that I have ever seen, and there are moments when you really are hanging onto the edge of your seat". (Cecil Wilson, *Daily Mail* 2nd June 64). "Familiar though we are with the spectacle of aircraft running the gauntlet of flak and crashing aflame into hillsides, it has rarely been photographed with such dramatic force".

In conclusion *633 Squadron* has gained immortality for being the medium to capture for posterity, the last occasion in which five examples of de Havilland's magnificent Mosquito

Let's Get'em Flying!

Mosquito Squadron

The Sequel

Spurred on by the successes of *633 Squadron Oakmont Productions* set about making a sequel, entitled *Mosquito Squadron*, the film would once again be distributed through *United Artists*, with filming due to commence during the summer of 1968. Hamish Mahaddie had been contracted to locate suitable aircraft for the production, as he had done five years earlier for *633*. Mahaddie actually owned B.35 serial RS712, which he had purchased after *633* from the *Mirsch Corporation*. However the number of Mosquitoes available to him was considerably less than before. Peter Thomas of the Skyfame museum was approached, for the loan of the collections' two Mosquitoes, RS709 and TA719, for a period of three months. RS709 had been purchased from *Mirsch* in 1964 as replacement for TA719 which had a very serious accident. Piloted by 'Rocky' Stone the aircraft crash landed after some single engined flying at Staverton. Damage was considerable, and although repaired to static condition it would have been unlikely that TA719 could be flown without considerable expenditure. RS709 was flown to Staverton during October 1964 and had been kept in excellent condition throughout the intervening year. The engines were regularly run, but the aircraft was not allowed to be flown due to the Air Registration Board policy in force at the time. Mahaddie then turned his attention to hiring TA634, a B.Mk.35 which was owned by Liverpool Corporation and kept in excellent condition at Speke airport. Mahaddie was also involved with the production of *Battle of Britain* on which filming had just begun, and he soon found that he had no time to devote to *Mosquito Squadron* and regrettably had to leave the production. Air Commodore Sir Allen Wheeler (RAF ret'd.) then became the films technical adviser. Wheeler had earlier been responsible for the aerial work in *Those Magnificent Men....* Wheeler appointed engineer Les Hillman to locate Mosquitoes which could be returned to flying status without too much difficulty. On the May 8th, Les Hillman travelled to Speke to inspect TA634. The aircraft was found to be in excellent condition, and a deal was struck for its use in *Mosquito Squadron*, provided that TA634 was brought up to Air Registration Board standards.

After much negotiation Hawker Siddeley allowed their T.III RR299 to join the film. Director Boris Sagal had four airworthy Mosquitoes, one static, plus a cockpit section available to him, a far cry from *633*. The screenplay, written by Donald S. Sanford and Joyce Perry, was loosely based on the Amiens raid of 1944, although for the film the prisoners were British, and their prison was only the secondary target. The real nature of the mission was for the fictitious 641 Squadron to destroy the German underground factory then manufacturing a new devastating 'V' weapon, with the use of *High Ball* type bombs. The underground facility was adjacent to the chateau, 'Charlon' where the PoW's were imprisoned.

The budget for *Mosquito Squadron* was considerably less than *633's*, and accordingly there were no established stars involved in the production. David McCallum *(Man from Uncle)* pictured above, took the lead role, and eventually becoming an established actor in the future. He was supported by a host of British actors many of whom were regularly seen on U.K. television screens at the time.

The various Mosquitoes were rapidly readied for their roles in various locations around the UK. At Staverton, RS709 was prepared for flight by staff from *Personal Plane Services* at

Top: Mosquito Squadron film poster (BFI Stills). Above: 633 Squadron camera ship NAA B-25J Mitchell contrasts with the Royal Aircraft Establishment Shackleton M.R.3 WR972 below, which was used as the camera platform for the filming of Mosquito Squadron (APN).

WARBIRDS WORLDWIDE
TWENTY NINE
52

Booker. They spent about a week preparing the aircraft ready for its film role. At Hawarden/Chester, RR299 was re sprayed on the 18th June and then flown to Bovingdon by Chris Capper three days later. Bovingdon was once again selected as the operating base and film set, due in the main to its proximity to the film studios. Over at Speke, Doug Bianchi (mentor of *Personal Plane Services*) was overhauling TA634. This took the best part of a month to complete, the aircraft finally being flown by the legendary Neil Williams on June 17th. This was the first time that Williams had ever flown a Mosquito; due to a number of circumstances the dual control T.III RR299 was not available, so Williams had to make do with looking over the shoulder of Taffy Rich (who flew in *633 Squadron*) in a B.35, although he did get some taxying practice in! Large crowds and the media had gathered at Speke to see TA634 fly. On landing back after the initial test flight a very relieved Williams stepped out of the cockpit, hoping that there weren't going to be too many searching questions fired his way. Later in the day TA634 departed for Bovingdon and Williams' log book was duly signed by Taffy Rich 'checked out'.

The four pilots selected to fly for *Mosquito Squadron* were Taffy Rich (who was approved by the Air Registration Board as type rated examiner for Mosquitoes), Neil Williams (a graduate of the *Empire Test Pilots School* and renowned aerobatic and display pilot), 'Dizzy' Addicott, then a test pilot with B.A.C. at Wisley (who had over 2000 hours logged on Mosquitoes during and after World War II, while in the RAF and Fleet Air Arm) and Pat Fillingham, a test pilot with Hawker Siddeley at Hatfield, who had a vast number of hours on type. Although the Squadron depicted in the film was renumbered it was decided that the aircraft would wear 'HT' codes, as in *633 Squadron*, so that various sequences could be re utilised in this sequel. The period of flying for the cameras was to be very short. TA634 made only six flights with a total duration of just seven hours and fifty minutes. RS709 was flown on a number of occasions over the Staff College at Minley Manor near Blackbushe in Surrey, which was portraying the Chateau 'Charlon'. These strafing runs, almost became too realistic, as during one of the sorties flown by Taffy Rich, a smoke canister fell off and set fire to Iver Heath near Slough - it took ten fire appliances to put out the blaze. The camera ship used in the production was the Royal Aircraft Establishment's Avro Shackleton MR.3 serial WR972 flown by Tom Sheppard - the aircraft was normally employed on parachute development work, including crew-escape and drag chutes for Concorde.

The memorable opening scene in the film, where the four Mosquitoes are shown approaching the coastline, was filmed near Scarborough behind the venerable 'Shack'. The Mosquitoes had positioned to RAF Coltishall for these sequences. The crash sequence from 633 Squadron involving RS718 was utilised in the final cut of *Mosquito Squadron*, along with various other short clips. The Skyfame Museum's non airworthy B.Mk.35 TA719 was transported to a field behind the MGM Studios at Borehamwood for a crash scene involving David McCallum, and regrettably TA719 was damaged again by some over enthusiastic special effects people, with the wing and fuselage catching fire. At the very end of the film two very dubiously camouflaged Avro Ansons were utilised as crew transports - these two aircraft were on loan from the Southern Communications Squadron, whose Ansons were due to retire very shortly.

After a very short period, the aerial unit disbanded, with RR299 returning to Hawarden, whilst the remaining B.35's were flown back in turn to their owners by Neil Williams. The final close up shots were filmed in the studio utilising the cockpit section of TJ118.

Mosquito Squadron was *not* a success at the box office and in many ways was marketed as a 'B' movie, often screened as part of a double bill or as a supporting feature. On the whole the lack of expenditure and poor script showed through. One aspect which severely effects the films credibility is in the model work and back projection which is inferior in many ways to *633 Squadron*; very reminiscent of war films from the early 'Fifties.

One redeeming aspect was that once again it did capture the sight and sound of four Mosquitoes in the air, a sight not likely to be repeated. "CUT"! WW Gary Brown.

Acknowledgments.
The author would like to thank James Kightly for BFI research, Peter and Ray Thomas, (without their input this article would not have been produced), Dizzy Addicot, Brian Stainer of *Aviation Photo News* for allowing us to use numerous photographs, Peter R March and Alan Croft for the loan of photographs and T.G.'Hamish' Mahaddie. A listing of all the aircraft utilised in these films will appear in WW30.

WARBIRDS WORLDWIDE

Purple Plain

633 Squadron and *Mosquito Squadron* were not, by any means, the only films made featuring the deHavilland Mosquito, though they were two of the three which were made as post-war feature films. The other film which had Mosquitoes present was a film entitled *The Purple Plain* starring Gregory Peck, and based on a story by H.E.Bates. A number of Mosquitoes were used, but the majority of the action took place after the Mosquito carrying the films stars crashed and burnt out.

During the War the Mosquito as one of the main aircraft in Britain's arsenal was to appear on a number of cinematic occasions, varying in veracity from the honest to the ridiculous.

On the Amiens Prison raid *(Operation Jericho)* one of the Mosquitoes carried cine cameras, and this was later released into the public domain. Though basic, even today, the silent, flickering images of those Mosquitoes attacking the Prison make for sober but interesting viewing. The Crown Film Unit made a short feature showing the Mosquito they did for most other aircraft, so that it could be used in recognition lessons for appropriate personnel from the Royal Observer Corps to the R.A.F. themselves. In Canada, a film was made called *Mosquito Squadron* by the National Film Board of Canada. From other sources, including deHavilland and the R.A.F. there is some fine footage also of Mosquitoes being made and flown which has cropped up in documentaries and retrospectives since. Possibly the most startling is the footage taken without permission, clandestinely, from the cockpit, of Mosquitoes in colour in 1944; this footage is available in the video *Mosquitoes Airborne* and makes for fascinating viewing.

It is an indisputable fact that the Mosquito is one of the most aesthetically pleasing of aircraft when filmed; it is a pity there are too few films which show off the Mosquito to its best advantage.
WW James Kightly.

Let's Get 'em Flying!

Hawker Fury - Continued from Page 47

was once again serviceable. John needed to return soon to the U.K. and decided to fly the Fury to Breckenridge the following day where the Manager had kindly offered hangarage. This was successfully accomplished and at the end of the Easter Holiday John put the Fury into storage at Breckenridge. In view of the fact that the Breckenridge environment was very hot and dusty John needed to acquire dust sheets and canopy/engine covers to keep the Texas sand and dust out of the aircraft apertures. A local Motel kindly provided a number of bed sheets from which covers were fashioned by John and Barbara to enable the Fury to be well wrapped up and sealed from the elements before the three of them returned to the U.K.

In August 1991 John and Barbara arrived back at Breckenridge to commence preparations for Shipping the Fury home. The first surprise was to find that one of the previously full wing tanks was now totally empty due to a small leak. The leak was duly fixed by John and work commenced towards getting the Fury shipped back to the UK.

Flying the Atlantic in the aircraft had been dismissed as an option by John and after careful consideration he opted to ship the Fury via a Roll on Roll off ferry which would involve the least amount of airframe dismantling. However RO/RO services from the U.S. to the U.K. are only available from a limited number of ports and the best service was available through the *Wallenus Line* who had a service from Brunswick, Georgia, to Southampton.

For those whose geographical knowledge of the U.S. is a little sketchy I should explain that Brunswick is over 1,000 miles from Breckenridge and so John had to plan for an initial 1000 mile ferry flight within the U.S., largely over unfamiliar territory, to deliver the Fury to the port of embarkation. An arrangement was made with an FBO in Brunswick to act as shipping and packing agents, dealing with all the Customs and Shipping requirements and also supervise the actual loading of the aircraft on to the ship.

The 1000 mile ferry flight from Texas to Brunswick was carried out in three legs in August 1991, via Monroe, Louisiana and Troy, Alabama. Amongst other things John discovered that his compass was 30 degrees out, leading to some serious thinking in the cockpit as to why the scenery didn't match the map! Despite having to avoid some heavy thunderstorms over Alabama, John arrived at Brunswick airport with the Fury safe and sound keeping the airport authorities happy with a low fly by on arrival in an aircraft they insisted on calling a Hawker Hurricane!

John was badly let down by his appointed FBO who suddenly decided that they didn't want to handle the Fury. Enquiries then began in a totally strange city, to find someone who would help him dismantle and ship a Hawker Fury out to the UK. Fortunately at this point one Buddy Edwards from Brunswick stepped in to help and was happy to take on the responsibility of setting up all the shipping arrangements.

The shipping company then decided, at the last minute, to take the scheduled ship off the service and replace it with a smaller one. The lower deck height in turn meant that the wings of the Fury had to be removed rather than simply folded. This resulted in a good deal of extra work without adequate support equipment. In the heat and humidity of Georgia this was no easy task. Once again John had business commitments back in the UK preventing him from remaining in Brunswick until the ship departed and so the support of Buddy Edwards was invaluable.

Before he left Brunswick for the UK John was able to lead a group of workers including his wife who set about preparing the Fury for its long sea voyage. The outer wings were mounted on to a catch cradle and trailer for later transport by road to the Dockside. John left the Fury in this state in the care of Buddy Edwards at Brunswick Airport and then returned to the UK. Approximately one week later Buddy towed the Fury 14 miles down public roads with a Police escort to the Docks and then put the aircraft into open storage on the dockside for three days, pending arrival of the Ferry.

I hope it has become clear that the purchase and subsequent shipping to the UK of the Fury was logistically a very major undertaking for a private individual. If the logistic problems were not enough there would now enter another major "hassle Factor" at Brunswick Docks - good old fashioned vandalism. It should be remembered here that at this time the Gulf conflict was at its height and the local Brunswick Press had somehow got wind of the fact that an "Iraqi Fighter plane" was in storage at the Docks.

One night reports were submitted by the Docks Police of gunfire in the area and Buddy Edwards rushed immediately to the Fury to find that local vandals had decided to take pot shots at it. Here the hand of good fortune stepped in - a number of shots had been reported but only one had struck the Fury and this had hit in the Port wing between two ribs, in front of the main spar. This damage, whilst extremely annoying, was nevertheless repairable - had the spar been hit then the aircraft would have been grounded.

The Fury was subsequently loaded on to the ferry by Buddy Edwards in September 1991 with outer wings off and the aircraft was securely tied down in the cargo hold standing on its undercarriage with the Prop tips just clearing the deck roof by a couple of inches. The Ferry sailed for the UK on September 1st 1991 and arrived in Southampton on September 21st having sailed via Charleston, Norfolk, New York, Boston, Le Havre, Antwerp and Gothenburg.

John and his team of Ron Collins, Gerry Bull, David Lloyd, Jed Mackie and Tony Miles were all there to meet the ship on its arrival in the U.K. After a couple of days for the completion of the importation formalities, customs clearance etc., the aircraft was ready to be towed out of Southampton Docks and up to Eastleigh Airport for refitting of the wings. Prior to this John had to obtain the agreement of the Dept. of Transport for towing the aircraft on Public roads, together with consents from County, Police and Highway Authorities. This procedure had taken some six months to negotiate. It should be remembered that the tip of the Prop is some 16 feet off the ground which required John to carry out a full survey of his planned route out of the Docks to the airport and fully satisfy the authorities that all bridges, trees, overhead cables etc could be safely cleared. To ensure minimum traffic disruption the Police insisted that the tow should

Continued on Page 56

Below: The Fury is a big, thirsty fighter - not for the faint hearted - seen here taxying out at Benson prior to a training sortie with John Bradshaw at the controls.

VINTAGE MILITARY AIRCRAFT

Do you need on-site assistance to access the wealth of technical information and historical data available at the USAF Museum, Dayton, Ohio?

- AIRCRAFT & SYSTEMS TECH ORDERS
- HISTORIES, MARKINGS & PAINT SCHEMES
- EXPERIMENTAL FIGHTERS & BOMBERS
- CAN PROVIDE IN 35mm, XEROX, VIDEO ETC.
- REASONABLE FEES BASED ON COMPLEXITY

This is a commercial service, offered by a retiree with 50 years pertinent experience. There is no official connection with the USAF Museum

WILLIAM C. LINDSAY
(513) 399 7540 USA

JRS

J R S ENTERPRISES, INC.

5475 NORTH COUNTY ROAD 18, MINNEAPOLIS, MINNESOTA 55442

Purveyors of Quality Aero Engines for Discerning People

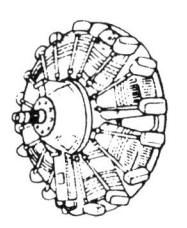

Call us with your needs or questions

Tel: 612/559-9457

We Specialize in Large Aircraft Engine Overhaul

FAA Repair Station No. 212-23
Covington Aircraft Engines, Inc.

Major Overhauled Engines
Specializing in Pratt & Whitney
R-985-AN1 or 14B
R-1340-AN1
R-1340-S1H1-G

P.O. Box 1344, Municipal Airport, Okmulgee, Okla. 74447, U.S.A.

Tel 918-756-8320 Fax 1-918-756-0923 Telex 3791814

Sample issues $4 each
1 year subscription $25
Overseas $30

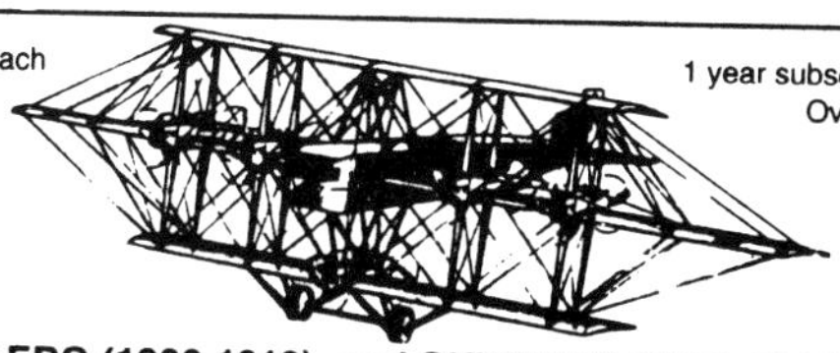

WW1 AERO (1900-1919), and SKYWAYS (1920-1940)
Two Journals for the restorer, builder, & serious modeller of early aircraft.

- information on current projects
- news of museums and airshows
- technical drawings and data
- photographs
- scale modelling material
- news of current publications
- historical research
- workshop notes
- information on paint/color
- aeroplanes, engines, parts for sale
- your wants and disposals

Sole distributors for P3V, a computer program to generate a 3-view from a photograph.

Published by: WORLD WAR 1 *Aeroplanes*, INC.
15 Crescent Road, Poughkeepsie, NY 12601 USA (914) 473-3679

WARBIRD PARTS & MEMORABILIA

Jay Wisler, 2710 Clark Road, Tampa, FL 33618, U.S.A.

World War II Aviation items for Sale. Armament, clothing and headgear, Oxygen equipment, parts for specific aircraft and much more. Send $2.00 for latest inventory. Tel/Fax 813 968 5048

HAWKER FURY continued from Page 54

only be undertaken at the quietest possible time on the Southampton roads - ie at the break of dawn on a Sunday morning. So, on the 29th September 1991 the team started the tow out of the Docks at first light (approx 06:45 hrs) on a Sunday morning. Typical British autumn weather was to prevail and for the whole tow on public roads it poured down with rain. In accordance with normal safety procedures it was necessary to have a fully qualified Pilot sitting in the cockpit throughout the whole operation and as John was leading operations from the road an instructor colleague sat in the cockpit for the entire journey, complete with brolly! The Police did a marvellous job stopping all other traffic, blocking off all road junctions ie taking the convoy through all red lights to complete the six mile tow in one hour twenty minutes. After arrival at Eastleigh Airport there was still plenty of time left in the day to refit the wings and prepare the aircraft for its transit flight to Wroughton. This time all the necessary trestles and ground equipment were to hand and the opportunity was also taken to fit all new wing attachment bolts. Speed tape was placed over the bullet hole in the port wing pending a permanent skin insertion repair which would follow when the aircraft was established at its U.K. operating base.

With regard to its operating base in the UK John initially chose Wroughton in Wiltshire - at first sight it may seem a relatively straightforward task to obtain an operating base for a desirable warbird but there are a number of important criteria that have to be satisfied - such as runway length and width, choices of take off direction according to wind conditions, hangarage and associated facilities, air traffic control, security and distance from John's and the ground crew's respective homes. Initially Wroughton worked well being a comparatively large airfield with long runways and an abundance of hangarage, but in July 1992 it appeared that the *Science Museum*, who manage the site, were wishing to adopt a policy which concentrated efforts on the development of Wroughton as essentially a static museum with flight operations being actively discouraged. Johns requirements were to regularly fly training sorties in the Fury in order to retain currency on type and so he needed a base where regular flight operations were feasible. He therefore opted to move the Fury to Benson during 1992 where he was flight instructing, and where 60 Squadron RAF kindly allocated space in their hangar.

Above: Pulling the prop through prior to moving the Fury outside **Left:** Fury cockpit is painted light grey and has a modern nav/comm fit

The rest of 1992 was spent flying, working up the Fury programme and taking care of engineering requirements before putting it out on the UK display circuit. He resisted the temptation to rush into display flying in the Fury and it wasn't until May 1993 when the Fury made its first public appearance at the Fighter Meet at North Weald, flying a combined display with Mark Hanna in the OFMC Fury.

N36SF had been worked on extensively by the *Coleman Museum* prior to the sale. John feels the Baghdad Furies were well looked after when placed in store by the Iraqis and his example went to Coleman with recorded engine hours of 195 and recorded airframe hours of 690. Bearing in mind that a well looked after civil operated Centaurus can go 6-700 hours before major overhaul John's Fury was quite a young aeroplane on acquisition and since then has completed a further 25 hours including the training John did on it in the U.S. prior to shipping to the UK.

During the overhaul at Coleman Kenny Day and his team did a sound job on the Fury, overhauling the airframe and all flying controls, replacing all the electrics, hydraulics and fuel systems and fitting totally new modern instrumentation. The cockpit fit included all new instrumentation, LORAN, VHF, VOR/ILS, ADF and a transponder with Mode C. (Altitude readout). Since purchase John has also fitted a GPS satellite Nav package. Further to this some 3000 man hours have been put into the aircraft since its arrival in the U.K. and it is now almost at the standard required by John of all his aircraft.

When the *Coleman Museum* received the aircraft the Centaurus engine had been inhibited - the cylinder heads were removed and the bores were full of inhibiting oil with the interior condition of the engine being very good. In view of this a total strip down of the engine was not necessary and so far John has been delighted with both its reliability and very low oil consumption. In the cruise at low rpm the Fury has been using less than one gallon of oil per hour rising to two gallons per hour as the rpm rises (with a typical display being flown at 2400 rpm and 38" of manifold pressure). It is operated using a specially formulated preservative oil recommended by a major Oil Company.

The structural condition of the Fury prior to its overhaul was also very good - the majority of the skins are original. A new zero time prop was fitted and the undercarriage totally stripped and overhauled with new brakes and tyres. When John first flew the Fury it had less than 8 hours on the engine following the completion of the Coleman inspection. However, he discovered an unacceptable high level of mag drop and this basic ignition problem was to plague the engine for some time until it was tracked down to faulty connectors. Once the ignition had been sorted out the engine was transformed in its characteristics and is now running very smoothly, developing ample power. John's normal practice is never to exceed 38 inches MAP even for take off.

Whilst it is clear that a major logistics exercise has to be launched and managed to ground support such a high performance aircraft one has also to put into perspective the direct operating costs. As far as insurance and other primary costs it should be borne in mind that the Centaurus Mk 18 burns approx 60 gallons per hour of Avgas in the cruise rising to 4-5 gallons per minute at take off power! Full combat power fuel burn is therefore running at the equivalent of nearly 300 gallons per hour - not for the faint hearted!

John has now worked up an exciting seven minute standard display sequence for the Fury, which in his words has been designed to show off the aircraft to its maximum benefit - not the pilots - and this is flown at 2400 rpm and 38 inches. During his standard display John will not pull more than 4 1/2g and he needs at least a 3,000 feet cloudbase for loops which are entered at not less than 280 knots. He always looks for at least 3,000 feet at the top of a loop and if this isn't on the clock will roll out as a precaution.

With regard to the future John is now looking forward to an active couple of years on the U.K. display circuit with this superb aeroplane but he realises that due to the logistics of operation, expense and time required to maintain the aircraft properly that he simply will not be able to carry on operating it regularly for many more years. In the meantime airshow enthusiasts in the UK and on the continent should continue to enjoy the sight of this most magnificent product of the former Hawker line and perhaps admire a fine example of what in the authors view is the finest production piston fighter ever built. **WW Richard Paver.**

The author would like to express his sincere thanks to John Bradshaw for his considerable assistance in making this article possible.

WARBIRDS
W O R L D W I D E

The Flying Insurance Broker

Lance Toland actively operates warbirds in the United States. His company, *Lance Toland Associates* insures more warbirds than any other company there - We find out why.......

*Top: Lance Toland with the Jet Provost T.3 N7075X before it was assembled. The aircraft was joined later by T.Mk.5 XW369 which is also now assembled and flyable. XW415 (which belongs to Wiley Sanders) is shown **below** at Griffin (Photo LTA)*

Lance Toland is a unique individual with many aims in life. In case you begin to feel this is a paid for sales pitch think again, for Lance Toland is the man behind *Lance Toland Associates* of Griffin, Georgia. *LTA* insure more warbird aircraft than any other company in the United States and in a recent interview I began to learn a little about the company's philosophy. Lance's philosophy is built on sound, often uncomfortable experiences.

Lance began in business by working for an insurance company in the property and casualty field. He became interested in vintage aircraft at an early age, helping to rebuild several before he himself acquired an ex Ghanaian DH Chipmunk which he restored himself in 1979. It was here that he experienced his first taste of what it is like when things go wrong. After being told he was insured on the Friday he flew the aircraft over the weekend before suffering an accident in the aircraft on the Sunday. After recovering from his injuries he found, to his cost that the aircraft *had not* been correctly taken on risk and so *he was not insured*.

Following this Lance continued with his aviation career and became a charter pilot on DC-3s. This belies an interesting story, for Lance was tasked with finding insurance coverage for the aircraft by his boss. After several days of research and making telephone calls Lance found the most cost effective way of insuring the DC-3, and saved the company a cool $65,000 into the bargain. May 15th this year will see this aircraft (the oldest DC-3 still flying and the sixth built) take up its 15th renewal with *Lance Toland Associates*. Lance also obtained his ATP rating whilst flying this aeroplane. He carried on flying for several years, keeping on the insurance agency as a part time venture until he had to make the decision whether to advance his career as an airline pilot or make Lance Toland Insurance a full time profession. He chose the latter.

Currently Lance owns two Beech Barons, a BAC Jet Provost T.Mk.3 and T.Mk.5 and a Pilatus T.3-05. So he is well versed in handling all the difficulties and beaurocracy involved in operating jet aircraft including the F.A.A., often seeking to over regulate the jet warbird movement at national level in the United States. This has, says Lance "made me even more determined to provide a high level of service to my customers. I have experienced for myself all the hassle, all the paperwork and regulations involved in maintaining and operating warbirds. So when it comes to getting aircraft insured I want to make sure that the owner can accomplish this easily, without hassle and feel comfortable that he is covered. We want to keep it as simple as possible." *LTA* has also set themselves another goal. To educate owners - essentially says Lance "...to ensure there are no misunderstandings. No misunderstanding about the contract and no misunderstandings about their coverage, so if something does happen the owner knows he is covered. After all you have the shiniest warbird, beautifully restored, expertly operated and pay the largest insurance premium, but if your insurance policy is not set up correctly......."

In the early days of operating the more exotic jets and the formation of the *Classic Jet Aircraft Association* Lance played an important supportive role using both his knowledge of aviation and his knowledge of insurance to maximum benefit for all involved. So when you go to *LTA* for insurance you know you will be talking to a knowledgeable fellow warbird owner. **WW Paul Coggan**

Let's Get 'em Flying!